FATHER**LESS**

WHAT IF THE ANSWER TO ALL THE PROBLEMS OF THE WORLD COULD BE SOLVED BY RESTORING CREATION BACK TO ITS CREATOR?

John C. Whitfield III   Kierra McKenzie

Unless otherwise indicated, all Scripture quotations are taken from the King James Version®.

Scripture quotations marked AMP are taken from the Amplified® Bible (AMP), copyright © 2015 by The Lockman Foundation. Used by permission. www.Lockman.org.

Scripture quotations marked CEB are taken from the Common English Bible (CEB), copyright © 2011.

Scripture quotations marked ESV are taken from the English Standard Version (ESV) of the Holy Bible, English Standard Version. ESV® Text Edition: 2016. Copyright © 2001 by Crossway Bibles, a publishing ministry of Good News Publishers. All rights reserved.

Scripture quotations marked NASB are taken from the New American Standard Bible®, copyright © 1960, 1962, 1963, 1968, 1971, 1972, 1973, 1975, 1977, 1995 by The Lockman Foundation. Used by permission. www.Lockman.org.

Scripture quotations marked NIV are taken from the New International Version (NIV), copyright © 1973, 1978, 1984, 2011 by Biblica.

First paperback edition, November 2019, Los Angeles, CA

Published by: Prolific Kingdom; Edited by: Mark Miller

Cover Design by: John Whitfield & Kierra McKenzie

ISBN 978-1-7340215-4-7

Library of Congress Control Number: 2019920877

www.prolifickingdom.com

DEDICATION

To God the Father, God the Son and God the Holy Spirit:

We are humbled and eternally grateful that You have given us the opportunity to write this book. We know without a shadow of a doubt that we could not have done it without You. As people read this book, they will immediately become aware that the words that they are reading did not come from the authors. The words of this book were divinely inspired and written as dictated from Holy Spirit. Each chapter, each revelation and every verse included were inspired, and they serve to restore the heart of the sons to the fathers, and the hearts of the fathers to the sons (Malachi 4:6).

When we were inspired, we wrote, and when Your Spirit lifted on what we were writing, we stopped. Writing this book with Kierra McKenzie has been a tremendous honor. Our synchronicity during the writing of this book has been truly amazing. We are keenly aware of the fact that "one man plants, another one waters, but God gives the increase" (1 Corinthians 3:6-9). We would not even plan a book-writing day, and we would be in two different cars going in two different directions — when the Holy Spirit would give us an unction (divine empowering inspiration). That unction would turn into a conversation where one of us would share a fresh revelation that Holy Spirit just downloaded. That revelation would then turn into a chapter title or topic that would then be unfolded for several paragraphs or pages.

While writing this book, God tuned in the way we hear His voice like never before. This is why we are dedicating this book to the Godhead, Three in One — for guiding us, inspiring us and giving us revelation after revelation to unlock the identity, purpose and destiny of every reader.

Visit us at www.prolifickingdom.com for Courses, Webinars, Books, Coaching, Videos, Updates, and Prolific Content!

TABLE OF CONTENTS

ACKNOWLEDGMENTS

This has been an unforgettable journey, beginning with one word from God to a book filled with numerous revelations for the end times. We are thankful to our family and friends, some of the first to have a chance to partner with us and believe in the commissioning of this book.

A part of that family is our beloved morning prayer family, who has stood in faith and prayers with us to release this great work of our Father.

We want to thank all our supporters around the world who have sown in resources and prayers to see this marvelous work come to life.

To our editor, Mark Miller, this book will have a lasting impact and effect on our readers because of your thorough skills and outstanding attention to detail.

Thank you again to all who have seen the hand of God on this message. We believe that each and every one of you will reap the harvest of every revelation that this book will bring to our generation — for the Glory of our God.

FATHERLESS

FATHERLESS NAVIGATION GLOSSARY

In order to help our readers get the most out of this book, we would like to explain some terminology. Our *Fatherless* Navigation Glossary is to help you better digest and retain the information you are about to receive.

Anointing – The equipment of gifting(s) entrusted to each individual to accomplish what God has called you to do. God's power on you to do what you couldn't do without him.

Calling – The divine, "God-given direction" for your life. The talents, passions and injustices that you hear on the inside of you calling out to be acted upon.

Container – Every human being is a container, a disciple who is conditioned to both contain and maintain a certain discipline. How we are built determines what we can or cannot contain or maintain.

Destiny – The path you walk that leads you toward the fulfillment of your specific calling in life. Destiny is your future mapped out.

Disciple – A person who has dedicated a high level of commitment to learning a discipline, usually by being mentored by someone who has already achieved this discipline.

God the Father – The Father of spirits and all creation.

God the Holy Spirit – The Comforter, Guide and Teacher of those who are called to be the sons of God.

God the Son – Jesus Christ, the Son of God who died to restore mankind to sonship.

Grace – Divine enablement of God to do what we could not do on our own. God's insurance policy.

Orphan Spirit – This term is not referring to children who have become orphans through the loss of a parent. It is the false mental contract of a son who has walked away from or never received the impartation of a father. This agreement leaves the soul empty of identity, purpose and self-worth. It may not be rooted in reality, but agreement with the Orphan Spirit makes this relational dynamic real for the person who does not feel like they have received the genuine love and acceptance of a father.

Purpose – Understanding and walking toward the reason why you were born. Every person who is born has a purpose for their existence, and realizing your purpose is what allows you to walk in the fullness of "life and it more abundantly." *(John 10:10)*

Salvation – Confessing with your mouth and believing in your heart that Jesus died for your sins, repenting of those sins and asking Jesus to be the Savior of your life. Not a onetime transaction but something that is walked out over time in relationship with God.

Sonship – The essence of identity that is imparted by a father. A father looks into the eyes of his son or daughter and tells them who they are, how important they are, and establishes a foundation of stability in their soul.

Spirit of Adoption – The restoration of a son who accepts the adoption and Love of God the Father, provided by the blood of His Son, Jesus Christ. The "Spirit of Adoption" is accepted in our hearts and transforms us, putting us in position to receive everything that God has in His inheritance for us.

FATHERLESS

Malachi 4:5 — "Behold, I will send you Elijah the prophet before the coming of the great and dreadful day of the LORD: [6] And he shall turn the heart of the fathers to the children, and the heart of the children to their fathers, lest I come and smite the earth with a curse."

Luke 1:17 — "And he shall go before him in the spirit and power of Elias, to turn the hearts of the fathers to the children, and the disobedient to the wisdom of the just; to make ready a people prepared for the Lord."

What it means to be Fatherless

Fatherlessness does not mean that you did not have a physical father in your home. Fatherlessness means that the world was catapulted into a state of darkness and chaos when we disconnected ourselves from our Creator, Father God. When we disconnected from God the Father, we were disconnected from our identity, our purpose and the image of who we are. God the Father is and has always been the source of all mankind. To be disconnected from God the Father is death and to be reconnected to Him is life and peace. Like a plant disconnected from the soil or a branch disconnected from a tree, we immediately begin to die when we are disconnected from God the Father.

Adam and Eve lived in the continual presence of God which is called His Glory. They were clothed in the Glory of God and this was their habitation. It is the opposite of what we know now. It is liberty, peace, freedom, creativity and the fullness of purpose and identity. The adversary of man, lucifer, knew that if he disconnected man from God, they would live in a perpetual state of sin. This is why the definition of sin is not to do something wrong, but to be disconnected from God by your choices and thinking. Sin is a mind frame, a decision and a choice. Everything in life is all about walking in life (connection to God) or death (disconnection from God).

God chose the relationship with our earthly father to be our grid for relationship with our heavenly Father. We are supposed to be able to correlate the attributes of God the Father by having a healthy relationship with our earthly father. So of course, the goal of satan is to destroy our grid for an earthly father in an attempt to keep us from ever understanding God the Father. Now we live in a world that tries to confuse the importance of a father in the household but in the making of a child it is essential. As you read this book it will introduce you to statistics and research that attribute almost every major problem in our world to fatherlessness.

Just imagine, if human beings are created with a mother and a father, then it is not ideal to raise a child without the father that was necessary to conceive it. It is naturally missing 50% of what it needs to be successful. Success is not measured by financial gain, world achievements or status, but it is the development of your soul. Now we see a world that has been greatly deprived of fathers for various reasons; brokenness, incarceration, financial issues, broken relationships or some type of misunderstanding of their value. This book will look at the remedy to what we believe to be the number one problem in our world, Fatherlessness.

INTRODUCTION

As soon as a baby is born, that baby opens his or her eyes and looks for the very first time at the two people who are going to give them the grid for life in this world. The father gives the child their ID card, tells them who they are, helps them discover their identity and shows them how to become that person. The mother's job is to nurture a child and love them into that identity. The dad shows the child strength, courage, confidence and endurance. The mom shows a child many variations of the same thing, but it is the father who teaches the child how to lead and be led. The male is more than a sperm donor; he is the ongoing embodiment and example of what a father is supposed to be.

Being a father is not a one-time contribution. It is an example that a child must look at so he or she can successfully receive the impartations necessary to grow into a healthy human being. Shortcut this process in any way and you have the world that we are currently looking at. A child without a father is like a ship without a compass, drifting wherever the tide of life takes it. According to research from just about anywhere you look, a child with a healthy example of a father will most often outperform a fatherless child.

So, how do we reclaim what we never received? How do we receive an impartation from a father who was never there?

The good news is that nothing in this world is ever truly lost; it is just misplaced for the person who learns to see through the eyes of faith. Life is going to try to lie to you and make you think that you are not enough. Life is going to try to tell you, "You didn't have a mother, you didn't have a father, you didn't even have a proper upbringing" — but God! God always had a plan, and nothing in your life was a coincidence. Wherever it looks like you had a deficit, there was already a supply hidden for you in Him.

Life is a journey of discovering all the missing pieces. In the physical world, it looked like you didn't have them, like you were lacking — but in the spiritual, there is a never-ending abundance and spiritual supply that you can birth into this world at any moment by faith. Just ask the Father, "Where are those things that I was missing in my life?"

As you read this book, you will discover, everything that appeared to be lack was really hidden for you on the pathway of maturation. This is the maturation that God had always intended for Adam and Eve, their offspring, and for all mankind. As you turn each page, you will discover where your pieces were hidden — and, most importantly, that you were never fatherless.

Statistics of Fatherlessness:
 ➢ According to 72.2% of the U.S. population, fatherlessness is the most significant family or social problem facing America.

➤ 57.6% of black children, 31.2% of Hispanic children, and 20.7% of white children are living absent from their biological fathers.
➤ 71% of all high school dropouts
➤ 71% of teenage pregnancies
➤ 85% of children with behavior disorders
➤ 90% of all homeless and runaway children
➤ 63% of youth suicide
➤ 85% of all youth in prison[1]

Financial Effects:
➤ Children in father-absent homes are almost four times more likely to be poor. In 2011, 12 percent of children in married-couple families were living in poverty, compared to 44 percent of children in mother-only families.[2]

Drug and Alcohol Abuse:
➤ Fatherless children are at a dramatically greater risk of drug and alcohol abuse.[3]
➤ There is significantly more drug use among children who do not live with their mother and father.[4]

Physical and Emotional Health:
➤ A study of 1,977 children age 3 and older living with a residential father or father figure found that children living with married biological parents had significantly fewer externalizing and internalizing behavioral problems than children living with at least one non-biological parent.[5]
➤ Children of single-parent homes are more than twice as likely to commit suicide.[6]

As we researched, we were overwhelmed with the astonishing statistics that we discovered. We found fatherlessness to be not only a problem on our planet but the number-one challenge facing our world on an epidemic scale. No matter who you are, fatherlessness affects you and your world directly or indirectly.

You may think that you are safe and secure in your family and upbringing, but every time we allow a child to grow up without the right identity, we create an orphan. A human being with an Orphan Spirit has a broken mentality and is now open to turn into what they believe they must become in order to survive. This is where criminals, rapists, thieves and all forms of brokenness are born. This lack of self-value denies the person with an Orphan Spirit the capacity to value life for themselves or anyone else. The evil part of this equation is that a human being, which should have a good nature based on its creation, has now become comfortable being less than its original purpose. So much so, in fact, that an individual's heart can become deformed to the place of thinking that their immoral and reprehensible behavior is justified.

The father is the light that must be imparted to every child, and if not, he or she is left open for the void to be filled with darkness. The father is the one in the family structure designed to impart value, identity and purpose into each member of his family. This book is designed to restore the hearts of the fathers to their children and the hearts of the children to their fathers, and to put our world in a position of course correction that will align itself with our Creator, God the Father!

We could spend our time trying to deal with the fruit, or we can instead deal with the root of the number-one problem we see in our world: fatherlessness.

CHAPTER 1: REBELLION

The First Rebellion

God the Father is sitting on His throne on Mount Zion, and the trumpet of war sounds. A rebellion has started. One of God's most anointed angels, lucifer, has organized the rebellion. Not only has this angel rebelled, but he has also convinced one-third of the angels to rebel against their God, their Creator and their Father.

> *Isaiah 14:12 — "How art thou fallen from heaven, O Lucifer, son of the morning! how art thou cut down to the ground, which didst weaken the nations! [13] For thou hast said in thine heart, I will ascend into heaven, I will exalt my throne above the stars of God: I will sit also upon the mount of the congregation, in the sides of the north: [14] I will ascend above the heights of the clouds; I will be like the most High. [15] Yet thou shalt be brought down to hell, to the sides of the pit. [16] They that see thee shall narrowly look upon thee, and consider thee,*

saying, Is this the man that made the earth to tremble, that did shake kingdoms; ¹⁷ That made the world as a wilderness, and destroyed the cities thereof; that opened not the house of his prisoners?"

Luke 10:18 — "And he said unto them, I beheld Satan as lightning fall from heaven."

The Fall of Man

The rebellion started in Heaven as lucifer marched against God and then was thrown down to earth like lightning. God now creates mankind and forms man in His own image: in the image of the Father, the Son and the Holy Spirit. God gives man dominion over the earth and commands him to replenish the earth and subdue it. Unknown to Adam and Eve, there is already an adversary — the enemy of God, satan — in the earth, waiting to sabotage their destiny and their purpose. God gave man the earth and authority over it, but He also gave him one command: not to eat from the tree of the knowledge of good and evil.

Genesis 2:15 — "And the LORD God took the man, and put him into the garden of Eden to dress it and to keep it. ¹⁶ And the LORD God commanded the man, saying, Of every tree of the garden thou mayest freely eat: ¹⁷ But of the tree of the knowledge of good and evil, thou shalt not eat of it: for in the day that thou eatest thereof thou shalt surely die."

Genesis 3:1 — "Now the serpent was more subtil than any beast of the field which the LORD God had made. And he said unto the woman, Yea, hath God said, Ye shall not eat of every tree of the garden? ² And the woman said unto the serpent, We may eat of the fruit

14

of the trees of the garden: ³But of the fruit of the tree which is in the midst of the garden, God hath said, Ye shall not eat of it, neither shall ye touch it, lest ye die. ⁴And the serpent said unto the woman, Ye shall not surely die: ⁵For God doth know that in the day ye eat thereof, then your eyes shall be opened, and ye shall be as gods, knowing good and evil. ⁶And when the woman saw that the tree was good for food, and that it was pleasant to the eyes, and a tree to be desired to make one wise, she took of the fruit thereof, and did eat, and gave also unto her husband with her; and he did eat."

Adam and Eve's disobedience took them out of alignment with God and put them in alignment with satan. Therefore, they were now subjected to the law of sin and death, which is the curse that causes us to fail because we are disconnected from God. This is the very thing that happened to Adam when God told him not to eat from the tree. He was literally telling Adam, "If you eat of this tree and disobey my command, you will be lost into rebellion." Rebellion is the place where satan lives. *The definition of sin is to be separated from God.*

The Sin Issue

Our basic religious instinct is to target the sin in a person, because this is what we've been taught in church: that sin separates us from God. The deeper truth of the matter is that sin is not the core root of what separates us from God; it is rebellion. Sin is just what people in rebellion do. We sin when we are in a state of rebellion against God. Rebellion is the root; sin is the fruit. Once we partner with satan, we come into agreement with the Spirit of Rebellion that he embodies. The word "cursed" means "empowered to fail." The word "blessed" means "empowered to prosper." Satan was cursed and therefore man fell under that curse because he agreed with the adversary. So then, Jesus Himself had to become a curse — to pay the price for our transgressions.

> *Galatians 3:13 — "Christ hath redeemed us from the curse of the law, being made a curse for us: for it is written, Cursed is everyone that hangeth on a tree."*

The first murder in the Bible happened when Cain partnered with the Spirit of Rebellion, just like his parents did previously.

> *Genesis 4:6 (AMP) — "And the LORD said to Cain, 'Why are you so angry? And why do you look annoyed? [7] If you do well [believing Me and doing what is acceptable and pleasing to Me], will you not be accepted? And if you do not do well [but ignore My instruction], sin crouches at your door; its desire is for you [to overpower you], but you must master it.' [8] Cain talked with Abel his brother [about what God had said]. And when they were [alone, working] in the field, Cain attacked Abel his brother and killed him."*

Notice that the Father Himself was conversing with Cain when He told him, "If you do not obey My instructions, sin crouches at the door, waiting for you." What sin is God the Father talking about? The sin of rebellion. When you look at rebellion, we don't want you to look at it as just a sin. We want you to see it as a tree. Every sin ever committed by man is just a fruit of rebellion. Many churches, leaders and Christians spend time fighting the fruit of sin, but in this end time (which is coming and now is), we will go straight to the root of our problem: rebellion.

The State of The World

Rebellion:

- Opposition to one in authority or dominance
- Open, armed and usually unsuccessful defiance of or resistance to an established government
- An instance of such defiance or resistance

Synonyms: disobedience, defiance, revolt, disorder, riot or insubordination.[7]

Does this definition sound and look familiar to you? Is it something you have seen in other people or even yourself? Or maybe it looks like the very world around you? Take a moment and think about your day yesterday. How many times have you seen this definition played out in just that one day? Is it too many to count? If I were to sum up the disposition of this world into one word, it would be REBELLION. What we see on a daily basis can be rooted back to this one definition. Rebellion fosters a need for control and power without any level of submission or accountability. People won't take guidance, instruction or wisdom. They want to be left to their own way, and if you don't agree with their way, you're a criminal. People want to become an expert before they have learned to become a student.

Within the context of rebellion, there is now no such thing as honor and respect for authority or position. This goes both ways: People who are in authority are not honoring their responsibilities, and people who are under that authority disregard and challenge their power. Children stand against their parents and guardians and then go into the world to reenact the same against any level of authority.

The state of rebellion puts us in a place where we experience the opposite of God's intent for us.

Rebellion is:

1. The opposite of destiny and purpose
2. The opposite of your calling and identity
3. The opposite of clarity and order, leading to confusion
4. Chaos and disorganization
5. The lack of honor and respect of authority
6. Disobedience, which "is as the sin of witchcraft" *(1 Samuel 15:23)*
7. The cause of curses, sicknesses and diseases

Attributes of a Son vs. Attributes of an Orphan Spirit

It may surprise you that you have been seeing the attributes of an orphan spirit your entire life but did not know how to characterize them. You've likely seen these attributes in yourself, in your family or in your friends, and you've had no idea what the root of the problem was.

There are many problems in our world that we try to handle by dealing with the fruit, but in this book, we will examine how to get to the root of the problem and possible remedies. When we look at the current state of our world — with wars, murder, corruption, sickness, disease, racism, hate and division — we are seeing fruit that come from the condition of fatherlessness.

When Adam and Eve rebelled against the command of God, they not only lost the paradise that they lived in, but they also lost the paradise (Kingdom of God) that lived inside of them. Adam and Eve would now be thrust into a world ruled by darkness, and these former children of God would now be fatherless. They were fatherless not by God's choice but by their own choice to partner and agree with the fallen angel and former son of God, lucifer. Adam and Eve went from knowing who they were, and understanding their identity, to being in total darkness. This darkness is a state that every person who has not been reconnected with the Father lives in. It is described in great detail in *Isaiah 59*.

> *Isaiah 59:1 — "Behold, the LORD's hand is not shortened that it cannot save; neither his ear heavy, that it cannot hear: ² But your iniquities have separated between you and your God, and your sins have hid his face from you, that he will not hear. ³ For your hands are defiled with blood, and your fingers with iniquity; your lips have spoken lies, your tongue hath muttered perverseness. ⁴ None calleth for justice, nor any pleadeth for truth: they trust in vanity, and speak lies; they conceive mischief, and bring forth iniquity. ⁵ They hatch cockatrice' eggs, and weave the spider's web: he that eateth of their eggs dieth, and that which is crushed breaketh out into a viper. ⁶ Their webs shall not become garments, neither shall they cover themselves with their works: their works are works of iniquity, and the act of violence is in their hands. ⁷ Their feet run to evil, and they make haste to shed innocent blood: their thoughts are thoughts of iniquity; wasting and destruction are in their paths. ⁸ The way of peace they know not; and there is no judgment in their goings: they have made them crooked paths: whosoever goeth therein shall not know peace. ⁹ Therefore is judgment far from us, neither doth justice overtake us: we wait for light, but behold obscurity; for brightness, but we walk in darkness."*

In these verses Isaiah takes us deep into the characteristics and attributes of sin. We have no idea what we are even doing most of the time when we are in sin because our eyesight becomes darkened, by us allowing more and more degradation in until we resemble a completely different person. I once heard a great man of God say, "Sin will take you further than you want to go and keep you longer than you want to stay."

> *Isaiah 59:10 — "We grope for the wall like the blind, and we grope as if we had no eyes: we stumble at noon day as in the night; we are in desolate places as dead men. [11] We roar all like bears, and mourn sore like doves: we look for judgment, but there is none; for salvation, but it is far off from us. [12] For our transgressions are multiplied before thee, and our sins testify against us: for our transgressions are with us; and as for our iniquities, we know them; [13] In transgressing and lying against the LORD, and departing away from our God, speaking oppression and revolt, conceiving and uttering from the heart words of falsehood."*

10 Attributes of an Orphan Spirit

1. Do not value themselves properly so they also cannot see you properly or value your place in their lives.
2. Have a Spirit of Poverty and live in a place of debt, lack, want and shortage.
3. Are jealous of others' success and secretly hope others around them do badly so they can feel better about their failures and shortcomings.
4. Are good starters but bad finishers, due to a fear of success deep within.

5. Secretly hate and mistreat those who love them because of self-hate.
6. Are tossed to and fro by their thoughts because they have identity issues.
7. Don't really know who they are, so they take on multiple identities in search of recognition.
8. Are very open to narcissism, vanity, arrogance, perversion or other lewd behavior because no father has spoken identity into their life.
9. Are thirsty for attention and the energy of acceptance, and they will do just about anything to get it.
10. Think about short-term pleasures with no real awareness of the long-term repercussions of their actions.

10 Attributes of a Spiritual Son or Daughter

1. Represents his or her family name proudly.
2. Has self-confidence because it has been spoken into them over time.
3. Is a man or woman of honor who properly values the lives of others.
4. Has peace inside and is temperate. Has no proclivity to anger, violence and murder.
5. Is obedient, humble and able to take and follow instructions.
6. Is a giver, a friend and a lover.
7. Is a good communicator.
8. Knows his or her value and will not allow you to treat them less than.
9. Is creative, talented, skilled and industrious.
10. Fearlessly stands up for what's right in his or her beliefs.

Right now I want you to take a deep breath. Fill up your chest with as much air as possible and breathe out slowly. I want you to know that it's OK for everything not to be alright. You don't have to pretend for anyone, you don't have to act and pull out your mask, but it's now time to come face-to-face with the unresolved issues of your heart.

The Image of God

God created mankind in His image, making them with three distinct parts: body, soul and spirit, which work together as one. The thing that distinguished man from everything else that God created was our ability to live not by instinct but by choice. God loved and honored the choice of His creation so much that He respected their choice to divorce themselves from Him. This choice broke off every covenant that they had with God and put them in covenant with the Orphan Spirit of rebellion. This is the current state of the world that we live in.

> *John 3:16 — "For God so loved the world, that he gave his only begotten Son, that whosoever believeth in him should not perish, but have everlasting life."*

God the Father — in His Omnipotence (all powerful), Omniscience (all knowing) and Omnipresence (everywhere at once) — already had a plan in place to restore His creation to Himself. It would be a plan of redemption, provided through the death of His only begotten Son, Jesus. Jesus' death would open the door for anyone who believes in Him to come through His obedience and be restored as a son of God.

Key Points

1. Rebellion began with lucifer. *(Isaiah 14:13-14)*
2. Adam and Eve's rebellion took them out of covenant with God and brought them into covenant with satan. *(Genesis 2:17)*
3. Sin is not the core root of what separates us from God; it is rebellion. Sin is just what people in rebellion do. We sin when we are in a state of rebellion against God. Rebellion is the root; sin is the fruit. *(Genesis 3:1-6)*
4. The world is in a state of rebellion with satan. *(1 John 2:15-17)*
5. Fatherlessness doesn't mean that you didn't have a physical father in your home. Fatherlessness means that the world was catapulted into a state of darkness and chaos when we disconnected ourselves from our Creator, Father God. *(Isaiah 59: 1-9)*

Notes

_____

_____

_____

_____

_____

_____

_____

_____

_____

_____

_____

_____

_____

_____

_____

_____

_____

_____

_____

_____

_____

Notes

_____

_____

_____

_____

_____

_____

_____

_____

_____

_____

_____

_____

_____

_____

_____

_____

_____

_____

_____

_____

_____

_____

Notes

CHAPTER 2: PURPOSE

Why Was Man Created?

God wanted sons who were made in His own image. The Bible calls the angels the sons of God. In *Genesis 6:2* and *Job 1:6*, the angels were called sons, but they were not made in the image of God like man was.

> *Genesis 1:26 — "And God said, Let us make man in our image, after our likeness: and let them have dominion over the fish of the sea, and over the fowl of the air, and over the cattle, and over all the earth, and over every creeping thing that creepeth upon the earth. [27] So God created man in his own image, in the image of God created he him; male and female created he them. [28] And God blessed them, and God said unto them, Be fruitful, and multiply, and replenish the earth, and subdue it: and have dominion over the fish of the sea, and over the fowl of the air, and over every living thing that moveth upon the earth."*

God created man in His image, and his purpose is to rule, reign and create the way God does. The primary relationship that the Bible speaks of between a man and God is that of a father to a son; it is the framework for every other relationship. Knowing your purpose as a son is like sitting in the driver's seat of life. Not knowing your purpose takes you out of position to drive effectively. You cannot drive the car from any other seat except the driver's seat. You cannot live out your purpose in life from any other seat except sonship. And that's the way the Father designed it. You cannot get life right unless you get being a son right. The first man that the Father created was a son, and therefore everything we do thrives from that place.

God created Adam as a son and began to teach him His ways. Meanwhile, satan watched jealously from the sidelines with a plan to sabotage Adam's sonship and thus take authority over the earth. When Adam disobeyed God, he immediately entered into a rebellion and came out of position with God, life and the authority that God gave him over the earth. Satan cannot create; he can only kill, steal and destroy what has been created. Satan is not the originator of any idea; he only takes them out of their proper context. He influences people by getting them to agree with his perverted thoughts, twisting their minds, bodies and purposes into an abomination of the original creation. A sign of a person under the Spirit of Rebellion is confusion, disorientation and the lack of accountability. The Spirit of Rebellion works in opposition to the Spirit of Agreement.

This is why a person who is in rebellion destroys the relationships around them:

a son to a father,

a brother to a sister,

> a husband to a wife,
> a student to a teacher,
> a citizen to a state or country,
> a people to a government
> a member to a congregation,
> a creation to a Creator.

God's original intent and identity for Adam and Eve was to be sons made in His image to rule and reign over the earth. They were to have dominion over the earth and subdue it. They had the power to accomplish God's purpose because God made them in His own image (identity), as we see in *Genesis 1:27-28*. Adam and Eve were made in God's image, and they were given their identity and purpose from God. They were literally made Kings and Priests over the earth.

The devil knew that in order for him to steal ownership over the earth, he had to get Adam and Eve out of alignment with God and in alignment with the Spirit of Rebellion. Satan is the author of rebellion, "the spirit that now worketh in the children of disobedience." God had warned Adam that the day he ate from the tree of the knowledge of good and evil, he would surely die. This death was not a physical death but rather a spiritual death that would eventually lead to a physical death.

The devil literally stole Adam and Eve's clothing. When God talks about clothing in the Bible, He is talking about our thoughts. Whether He's talking about a robe of righteousness or dirty rags, He's talking about how we think. Adam and Eve's first set of clothing was given to them by God. It was the word of His authority to have dominion and reign over the earth. It was a glory covering them that they walked in, which was so thick that they didn't even know they were naked. This was their purpose.

When they entered into rebellion by disobeying God, they lost their clothing, and satan put it on and became the god (little "g") of this world. Adam and Eve were now left in the Garden of Eden (the Garden of Promise), naked, with no clothing. What were they clothed with before? The Glory of God! In the Glory is the authority, the Kingdom and the culture of Heaven. To die is to be cut off from your Kingdom supply.

The world is currently in the most incredible state of confusion that I have ever seen it in. Never in my life did I ever imagine a day where people don't know what bathroom to go into. This has nothing to do with gender but instead a society that has lost its way. When fathers stop speaking to sons, sons get lost in a world full of media, music, billboards and Instagram posts. Men walk around with question marks over their heads, asking who they are. Israel became a powerful nation because God the Father told Abraham who he was, Abraham then told Isaac who he was and Isaac told Jacob who he was. Because the forefathers spoke identity into them generation after generation, no matter how much captivity the people of Israel were in, they always rose to a place of power and influence because they knew who they were. What is now missing from the Church and Israel's completion is found in Romans:

> Romans 10:1 — "Brethren, my heart's desire and prayer to God for Israel is, that they might be saved. ² For I bear them record that they have a zeal of God, but not according to knowledge. ³ For they being ignorant of God's righteousness, and going about to establish their own righteousness, have not submitted themselves unto the righteousness of God. ⁴ For Christ is the end of the law for righteousness to everyone that

believeth."

What Is Your Purpose?

Many people question what their purpose is. How do you find your purpose? You are living, but you're not really alive until you find the reason for your existence. What question is the world asking that you are the answer to?

1. Why are you here?
2. If time and money weren't an issue, what would you do?
3. What would you wake up early and go to sleep late doing?
4. What is it that you do effortlessly that others find hard?
5. What gifts and talents do you have that others have highlighted to you?
6. What is it that you do that has a huge impact on others?

Have You Found Your Purpose Yet?

Purpose is not what you do — it's who you are. You are not separate from your purpose! You were created for the very purpose that you are called to. Thinking that you are separate from your purpose is like a lion saying to itself, "I'm trying to become a lion so that I can rule over the animal kingdom." But he is already a lion! He's not trying to become a lion. What needs to change is his perception of himself. Because the fact is that he will never *not* be a lion, but he can stop hanging around lions and doing what lions do because of his own perspective and self-image.

Your self-image can keep you from your purpose, but know that your purpose is not something that comes to you

— it is something in you that needs to be unveiled. Do not look to the world to tell you who you are. Once you discover your purpose, the world will now be attracted to it. Your God-given purpose will always have a place and be an answer to a problem in the world.

It Is Dangerous to Not Know Who You Are!

You may be a 100-percent-capacity person when it comes to energy, but you are living in a 25-percent-capacity life. So you feel crazy sometimes because you have an abundance of energy, imagination, creativity, drive and ambition, yet you are living a life that doesn't fit that capacity. But then when you get in position and you are fully living out your purpose, everything inside of you is going to find its proper place.

If you currently live in a situation where you feel unfulfilled, it's because you're not fully living out your purpose. This is the danger of living just to pay bills, living to exist and not understanding your purpose. A person who does not understand their purpose can easily get tricked into living a life below their calling.

Listen to your heart right now: What calling do you hear on the inside of you calling out to be fulfilled? What do you daydream about? What visions come to your mind when you are still?

Consumer vs. Creator

Once you have discovered your purpose, you are now in a position to become a creator and not just a consumer. The world creates, thrives off of and perpetuates consumerism. The trick of this world is to keep you consuming so that you are always in need, instead of in abundance. The Bible says:

John 10:10 (AMP) — *"The thief comes only in order to steal, kill and destroy. I came that they may have and enjoy life and have it in abundance [to the full, till it overflows]."*

You will never have abundant life if all you do is consume. But if you discover your purpose, you can create and enjoy the abundance as others consume what you have created.

What can you create? Is it a dance? A song? A book? An idea? An invention? Is it a skill or a trade?

We all have been given a gift. Our God-given gifts are given to us in order to fulfill the purpose for which we have been sent to this earth. As we use our talents we bring God glory by multiplying what He has given us by reason of use.

Matthew 25:24 (AMP) — *"The one who had received one talent also came forward, saying, 'Master, I knew you to be a harsh and demanding man, reaping [the harvest] where you did not sow and gathering where you did not scatter seed. ²⁵ So I was afraid [to lose the talent], and I went and hid your talent in the ground. See, you have what is your own.' ²⁶ But his master answered him, 'You wicked, lazy servant, you knew that I reap [the harvest] where I did not sow and gather where I did not scatter seed. ²⁷ Then you ought to have put my money with the bankers, and at my return I would have received my money back with interest. ²⁸ So take the talent away from him, and give it to the one who has the ten talents.' ²⁹ For to everyone who has [and values his blessings and gifts from God, and has used them wisely], more will be given, and [he will be richly supplied so that] he will have an abundance; but from the one who does not have [because he has ignored or disregarded his blessings and gifts from God], even what he does have will be taken away. [30] And throw out the worthless servant into the outer darkness; in that place [of grief and torment] there will be weeping [over sorrow and pain] and grinding of teeth [over distress and anger]."*

God is a God of love, joy, peace and understanding, but He is also VERY serious about His investments. God is intentional about purpose, fruit and multiplication. This parable also reveals what happens when we compare what we have to what someone else has. The last servant saw what the others received and was so discontent with his portion that he decided it wasn't worth doing anything with it. Never despise what you have or be ungrateful for what you have been entrusted with.

God is so serious about fruitfulness that Jesus cursed the fig tree in *Mark 11*, when He saw that it had no fruit.

Mark 11:12 (AMP) — "On the next day, when they had left Bethany, He was hungry. [13] Seeing at a distance a fig tree in leaf, He went to see if He would find anything on it. But He found nothing but leaves, for it was not the season for figs. [14] He said to it, 'No one will ever eat fruit from you again!' And His disciples were listening [to what He said]."

This piece of Scripture gives us insight into the ways of God. God hides things for a season of preparation and growth until they are ready to be revealed. What God is trying to show us is that nothing should be seen if it has nothing to offer. If that fig tree was visible from far off with all the physical features of looking like it was ready, but when you got up to it and it had nothing to offer, it was an abomination! You should be able to tell when someone or something is in preparation and when it's not. So, when it looks like it's ready but really isn't, then it has given a false presentation. And that is not of God. God makes it clear when something is ready and when something is not.

Key Points

1. Lucifer and the angels were also considered sons of God. They were not made in the image of God in the same way that Adam was, but the Bible refers to them as the sons of God. *(Job 2:1)*
2. God created man in His image, with the purpose to rule, reign and create the way that God does. *(Genesis 1:26-28)*
3. We cannot create our own righteousness; we must submit to God's. *(Romans 10:1-4)*
4. Jesus' purpose is to give life and give it more abundantly. Satan's purpose is to kill, steal and destroy. *(John 10:10)*
5. What question is the world asking that you are the answer to? Purpose is not what you do — it's who you are. You are not separate from your purpose!
6. God is very serious about purpose. *(Matthew 25:13-30)*

Notes

_____

_____

_____

_____

_____

_____

_____

_____

_____

_____

_____

_____

_____

_____

_____

_____

_____

_____

_____

_____

_____

_____

Notes

_____

_____

_____

_____

_____

_____

_____

_____

_____

_____

_____

_____

_____

_____

_____

_____

_____

_____

_____

_____

_____

Notes

_____

_____

_____

_____

_____

_____

_____

_____

_____

_____

_____

_____

_____

_____

_____

_____

_____

_____

_____

_____

_____

_____

_____

CHAPTER 3: THE KINGDOM OF GOD

The Family Blueprint:

God began a covenant with Abraham that would be the blueprint for all mankind. So much so that He said that all those who belong to Christ "are Abraham's seed, and heirs according to the promise" *(Galatians 3:29)*.

> *Genesis 17:1 — "And when Abram was ninety years old and nine, the LORD appeared to Abram, and said unto him, I am the Almighty God; walk before me, and be thou perfect. ²And I will make my covenant between me and thee, and will multiply thee exceedingly. ³And Abram fell on his face: and God talked with him, saying, ⁴As for me, behold, my covenant is with thee, and thou shalt be a father of many nations. ⁵Neither shall thy name any more be called Abram, but thy name shall be Abraham; for a father of many nations have I made thee. ⁶And I will make thee exceeding fruitful, and I will make nations of thee, and kings shall come*

out of thee. ⁷And I will establish my covenant between me and thee and thy seed after thee in their generations for an everlasting covenant, to be a God unto thee, and to thy seed after thee. ⁸And I will give unto thee, and to thy seed after thee, the land wherein thou art a stranger, all the land of Canaan, for an everlasting possession; and I will be their God."

The father of faith, Abraham, would pass down a message to his son Isaac that would then be passed down to *his* son Jacob. The promises were given by God and would have to be transferred from generation to generation. This is the way of God. This is the blueprint of God: for a father to get the promises from God, look into his son's eyes, tell him who he is and continually remind him of the promises so that he would walk them out.

This is one of the greatest reasons for the position and power that Israel and Jewish people have, because they understand the promises of God and they pass them down from generation to generation. No one has to look for their identity; no one has to go searching for their purpose. It has been handed down to them from one generation to the next.

If you want to find brokenness in the world, look for a person or a group of people who do not know who they are. A generation that doesn't know who they are, hasn't been told who they are from the generation before them. In the absence of fathers speaking into you, there comes media, culture and a society telling you who they want you to be.

The Container

We want it to be 100-percent clear that we believe that both mothers and fathers are equally important in the physical, emotional and spiritual makeup of a child. It is important to know what we are creating. A child is like a container, and both a mother and a father are continually adding to this container. The substance that a mother pours into this container is different from the substance that a father pours into this container. They are not pouring the same substance, which is why it is ideal to have both a male and a female perspective pouring into a child. When one parent is missing, it definitely affects what kind of container is being produced. Ask any child that is a product of a single-parent home or a divorce if the loss of one of their parents had an effect on them, and you're more than likely to hear a "yes."

What we see today in our generation are containers that are oftentimes unable to hold certain ingredients of life because of how their container was produced. With bullying, social media harassment and rising suicide rates, we are hearing more and more stories each day of a generation that has not been prepared for the pressures of social interaction. We have to examine where we are as a society and how we got there. How do we get from a life of just existing to a place where we live in abundance?

The Heart

> *Jeremiah 17:9 — "The heart is deceitful above all things, and desperately wicked: who can know it?"*

There are certain parts of your heart that still look at God with unsurety. You believe Him partially but not completely. People are good pretenders. Some of the best actors are not in Hollywood but in the church. We are good with covering things up and not dealing with them. It's easy to say "Amen" when everyone else says "Amen." It's easy to say "Hallelujah" when everyone else says "Hallelujah." That's because we are trained to conform and not to be transformed.

In order to be transformed by the renewing of your mind, you have to give God full access to your heart. We all know that there are some places in our hearts that we have a "do not disturb" sign on. We're saying, "Jesus, You can go everywhere else except this room right here." Whether it's pride, unforgiveness, bitterness or offenses, somewhere in your heart you have decided that those doors are not allowed to be opened.

Your heart is not just inside of you; it is outside of you. What do we mean by that, you might ask? Inside of your heart are things that need to be worked on. You can't work on them all at once, but life is guiding you just like the veins in your heart. The veins are roads leading you to different places in your heart that need dealing with at certain times. Wherever you are in your heart, life is about to introduce you to people, circumstances or situations that will make you deal with unresolved heart issues. There are no coincidences in your life, only appointments and opportunities to change.

Now here's the tricky part: God is not going to make you change. He's just going to bring you to the crossroads and make sure you get to your appointments on time. Hint, hint: There are certain things that God will wink at for a certain period of time — but when it's time for promotion, it's time for devotion.

When you have unresolved issues in your heart, someone can be talking to you and trigger the brokenness that's inside of you. And then you're no longer talking to that person — you're talking to the people who hurt you before, as your unresolved issues come to the surface. You are having a conversation with a friend, a brother, a boss or anyone you are in a relationship with; they say something to you that seems totally innocent to them, but to you a bandage is lifted and a scar is exposed. This is the conversation you begin to have inside of your own heart as you come face-to-face with your brokenness. Your heart will always try to protect you even if it has to lie to you, but realize that this life is a game that God is sovereign over and in control of at all times. The development of our soul is the primary goal.

The Rich Young Ruler

> *Luke 18:21 — "And he said, All these have I kept from my youth up. ²² Now when Jesus heard these things, he said unto him, Yet lackest thou one thing: sell all that thou hast, and distribute unto the poor, and thou shalt have treasure in heaven: and come, follow me. ²³ And when he heard this, he was very sorrowful: for he was very rich. ²⁴ And when Jesus saw that he was very sorrowful, he said, How hardly shall they that have riches enter into the kingdom of God."*

An offering is what you want to give God; sacrifice is when God asks you for something that you weren't prepared to give Him. A sacrifice is a higher-level spiritual transaction with God, and it will always cost you something that is important to you. What is on the throne of your heart that God is asking you for?

Kingdom Alignment

> *Matthew 6:9 — "After this manner therefore pray ye: Our Father which art in heaven, Hallowed be thy name. [10] Thy kingdom come, Thy will be done in earth, as it is in heaven. [11] Give us this day our daily bread. [12] And forgive us our debts, as we forgive our debtors. [13] And lead us not into temptation, but deliver us from evil: For thine is the kingdom, and the power, and the glory, forever. Amen."*

Jesus and His forerunner, John the Baptist, proclaimed to the people, "Repent, for the Kingdom of Heaven is at hand." This declaration meant that there was a new operating system available for mankind.

The Kingdom of Heaven (Jesus' Operating System)
- ➤ Love
- ➤ Joy
- ➤ Peace
- ➤ Patience
- ➤ Hope
- ➤ Liberty
- ➤ Health
- ➤ Abundance
- ➤ Healing
- ➤ Spirit of Adoption

Adam and Eve started out with God's operating system. They were born in the Kingdom, they lived in the Kingdom and they were taught in the Kingdom from the very beginning.

What is the Kingdom? This word is tossed around all the time without people truly knowing what it means. The

Kingdom is God's family. God is the King, and those who are a part of God's family are the Kingdom.

Unfortunately, the assumption is that as soon as you pray for salvation, you are 100 percent in the Kingdom. Salvation gives you the opportunity to become a son, but creation is still groaning for your manifestation *(Romans 8:19)*. Sonship is something that must be worked out with fear and trembling. Many are called to it, but few are chosen. Discipleship is just a fancy word for sonship training. Now imagine how many Christians pray for salvation but have not received proper discipleship. This is why we have a world full of Christians but not a world full of the Kingdom. A world full of Christians only means that we have a world full of religion. A world full of true sons and daughters who walk in the Kingdom will display what Jesus displayed. Once we come to the fullness of this revelation, we are now in a position to do what Jesus did — and greater *(John 14:12)*. We will do greater works than Jesus because now instead of one Son, God will have many sons.

> *John 12:24 — "Verily, verily, I say unto you, Except a corn of wheat fall into the ground and die, it abideth alone: but if it die, it bringeth forth much fruit."*

Rebellion (the Cursed Operating System of satan)
- Fatherlessness
- Violence
- Poverty
- Debt
- Lack
- Want
- Sickness/Disease
- Fear

➢ Infirmity
➢ Orphan Spirit

The Orphan Spirit is literally the rebellious spirit of satan. When he was in Heaven, his name was lucifer and he was a very high-ranking son of God. Because of his beauty, giftings, talents and influence, the Bible says that he was corrupted and rebelled against God *(Isaiah 14:12-17)*.

In the previous chapters we showed how satan rebelled against God and convinced one-third of the angels to follow him in his attempt to overthrow God. As we see in **Luke 10:18**, Jesus was talking to His disciples and told them: *"I beheld Satan as lightning fall from heaven."* Before Adam and Eve were created as sons of God, He also called the angels His sons. They were not made in the image of God like we were, but the Bible still refers to them as sons:

Job 1:6 — "Now there was a day when the sons of God came to present themselves before the LORD, and Satan came also among them."

Why is this important? Because the first creations that God called sons had a rebellion against Him that was led by lucifer. The rebellious fallen angel that convinced one-third of the angels to rebel against God and lose their home and position in Heaven is the same one who convinced Adam and Eve to rebel against their Father and lose both their home in the Garden of Eden and their position as sons of God. As we mentioned earlier, sin is to be separated from God. Forget any religious connotations that you have surrounding the word "sin." Sin is the state of being separated from your Father by a different way of thinking. So, how did satan deceive mankind into rebelling against

God? He introduced doubt into the relationship, and through the door of doubt, deception was able to sneak in and set the stage for rebellion. How does the devil get us to rebel against God? Exactly the same way!

The Nature of the Devil

The nature of the devil is evil. This is not a spooky definition as you may have previously thought of the devil. "*De*-vil" and "*e*-vil" mean to divide, separate and pervert the original intent of something. When Adam sinned against the Father, he separated himself from the Father. To separate yourself from the Father is to partner with the devil, the evil one. The purpose of the devil is to divide you from something that God wants you to have. The devil's main goal is to divide you from relationships, from health, from prosperity, from God the Father, and he does that by dividing you from yourself.

What do we mean by "dividing you from yourself"? Getting you to question your identity and doubting your purpose. The devil tricks us by interjecting questions into our mind. While tempting Jesus in the wilderness, the devil already knew that Jesus was the Son of God, so his tactic was to get Him to question the truth. "If you are the Son of God, turn these stones into bread" *(Luke 4:3)*. If the devil can get you to question the truth, he can slide in some doubt. If he can get you to doubt, he can get you to fear. And if he can get you to fear, then he has you. Now you are on the other side of love. Faith works by love, but fear paralyzes. So the devil's goal is to paralyze us, thereby keeping us from carrying out what God called us to do.

James 1:13 — "Let no man say when he is tempted, I am tempted of God: for God cannot be tempted with evil, neither tempteth he any man: [14] *But every man is tempted, when he is drawn away of his own lust, and enticed.* [15] *Then when lust hath conceived, it bringeth forth sin: and sin, when it is finished, bringeth forth death."*

Let's look at these Scriptures this way: "Let no man say when he is <u>separated</u> from God, 'I am <u>separated</u> from God **by** God.'" This means there is nothing in God that makes Him separate Himself from us; it is the things that are in *us* that lure us away from God. This is called temptation.

Romans 8:35 — "Who shall separate us from the love of Christ? shall tribulation, or distress, or persecution, or famine, or nakedness, or peril, or sword?"

We are never separated from God because of anything that God does, so whatever attempts to separate us from God are a lie sent from the pits of hell on assignment from satan. It is time for us to stop looking at the devil as this big scary thing with so much power. The devil's power comes in his ability to deceive. The devil literally has to get *us* — the ones with the power and authority — to come into agreement with him and his lie in order to empower it.

We have to understand our responsibility in our relationship with God. How many times have you heard "If God wanted this to happen, it would happen"? This is not how it works! God has created a world based on free will, with the purpose of teaching us to discern between good and evil. Not by biting a fruit but by walking out a relationship between a father and a son. A son learns how not to be tempted by coming into alignment with the desires of his father. This requires an incredible amount of humility, which almost seems alien in this day and age.

Think of Isaac and how much humility and sonship it took for him to allow Abraham to tie him up and place him on the altar as an offering. There was no struggle, no fight, and no resistance. Knowing the nature of the devil is pivotal for helping us to understand the nature of God and our relationship to Him. Religion and media have made the devil WAY too big and our God WAY too small. The devil is a created being and cannot in any way compare to the power of God.

That's why a person operating in an Orphan Spirit doesn't mind stealing from you, for they are operating in the nature of satan himself. The nature of satan is to steal, kill and destroy. That's just what he does! So, when you see a world moving in that nature, you see a world being influenced by satan and his Orphan Spirit. You're watching an earth that has become an orphanage. The world without the Father is just an orphanage in operation.

God's Original Intent for Israel

God's desire for Israel was for them to become sons. Israel was and is God's chosen people. As we read earlier, God made a covenant with Abraham to make him a Father of many nations *(Genesis 17:5)*. After Joseph died, Israel found themselves slaves, taken into captivity into Egypt. God went to the adoption agency of mankind and chose a people for Himself. He adopted them out of the slavery of Egypt. He told Pharaoh to let them go and brought them out with a mighty hand — with the intention of them becoming sons, His family. God's desire for the children of Israel as they walked from Egypt to their Promised Land was for them to learn how to become sons. On their way, Israel was supposed to learn how to trust, depend on, communicate with and love God the Father as Daddy God.

As we see in **Hebrews 3**, most of the Israelites who were rescued out of Egypt died in the wilderness. Only a remnant made it into the Promised Land that God had prepared for them as an inheritance. Israel is a shadow or type of the Church. The story of Israel as depicted in **Hebrews 3** is an example of what could potentially happen to the Church if we choose not to live out our calling as believers and sons of God.

> *Hebrews 3:8 — "Harden not your hearts, as in the provocation, in the day of temptation in the wilderness: ⁹ When your fathers tempted me, proved me, and saw my works forty years. ¹⁰ Wherefore I was grieved with that generation, and said, They do alway err in their heart; and they have not known my ways. ¹¹ So I sware in my wrath, They shall not enter into my rest.) ¹² Take heed, brethren, lest there be in any of you an evil heart of unbelief, in departing from the living God."*

The book of Hebrews issues a sharp warning for us to search our hearts diligently for unbelief. This is the systematic hardening of our hearts even after we have experienced the goodness of God. We have the choice of whether we will remember the goodness of God that has brought us out of darkness, or whether we will mumble and complain about the things that we have not yet obtained. As they walked through the wilderness of life, the children of Israel were being tested to see what was in their hearts.

Unless You Become...

> *Matthew 18:1 — "At the same time came the disciples unto Jesus, saying, Who is the greatest in the kingdom of heaven? ² And Jesus called a little child unto him, and set him in the midst of them, ³ And said, Verily I say*

unto you, Except ye be converted, and become as little children, ye shall not enter into the kingdom of heaven. [4] Whosoever therefore shall humble himself as this little child, the same is greatest in the kingdom of heaven."

In these verses, Jesus was answering the disciples' questions, knowing that their intentions were wrong because they were trying to figure out who was going to sit at His right hand and His left hand. Jesus was showing them the doorway to the Kingdom of God: to pour yourself out so that He can fill you with His intentions, motives and directions.

To give them a grid for what this looks like, Jesus brought a little child before Him. Imagine this for a moment: You are a grown-up, an adult, and Jesus brings a little child in front of you and says, "I want you to be like this." What does that mean? God has a plan for us, a purpose for us, and we can't get to that destination unless we are willing to yield and follow Him. We literally have to abandon what we think, what we want and what we know — and trust the One who is leading us.

Jesus is the definition of sonship. When He took that little boy by the hand and brought him in front of the multitude, He was effectively showing an example of Himself, of the Kingdom and of what access to that Kingdom looks like. Jesus removed everything from Himself — honor, glory, reputation — and became like a little child willing to be led by the Father. This is why He is The Way. This is why He said that "there is no way to the Father but by the Son" *(John 14:6)*, meaning His example is what we must become.

This principle is important because it teaches a man how to follow God, and it also teaches a woman how to follow a man. The truth of the matter is that whether we are male or female, we all have to follow someone sometimes. This is the natural order of things, and there is no shame in being submissive to the right leadership. That doesn't mean you are going to agree with every decision made by the leader that God puts over you. Whether that's in a church or in a relationship. The ability to follow and be submissive is what makes us sons who God can use.

For example, in **Genesis 22:1-19**, Isaac had to follow Abraham, not knowing exactly what his plan was but trusting his father's relationship with God and his own relationship with his father. We are not always going to see the big picture right away, but we have to be obedient in the moment, walking by faith (relationship) and not by sight.

Led by the Spirit

The Holy Spirit just asked me the most amazing question: "Do you know the way back to Heaven?" When He asked me that, I immediately knew what He was talking about. That little child who Jesus pulled up in front of a crowd, he was the key — the gateway to getting back to the Kingdom of Heaven. Jesus said, "Unless you become like this, you will never enter the kingdom."

If I asked you to be quiet right now, could you do it? If I asked you to be still right now, could you do it? If I asked you to follow me right now, could you do it? This is what a child has to be ready to do at all times. He has to be willing to hear, to listen and to be led. The experiences that he collects during childhood teach him how to make decisions on his own when he is no longer a child.

This is the pathway to being led by the Spirit of God. The Bible tells us not only to be led by His Spirit but to be filled with Him. If a person is filled with wine or alcohol, you know it right away because they show the symptoms of someone who is drunk. Someone who is filled with the Spirit of God will show the symptoms of the Kingdom of Heaven.

> *Romans 8:14 — "For as many as are led by the Spirit of God, they are the sons of God."*

Fear belongs to bondage just as faith belongs to freedom. "Where the Spirit of the Lord is, there is liberty" (freedom). When we are being led by His Spirit, we will feel His freedom or liberation. When we are not walking in the Spirit, we will feel a spirit of bondage, which is fear. Fear is the climate of the world that we currently live in, and the only thing that can liberate us from that is the Holy Spirit. Many people call themselves Christians because "many are called, but few are chosen." How does God choose the "chosen"? Who's willing to be led? Who's willing to follow? Who's willing to obey? The answer to these questions is where God finds His sons. It sounds really easy until you realize that Jesus Himself had to learn obedience.

> *Hebrews 5:8 — "Though he were a Son, yet learned he obedience by the things which he suffered; And being made perfect, he became the author of eternal salvation unto all them that obey him."*

The Voice of God

A pivotal step that I feel is not emphasized enough in the church is learning the voice of God. Once you tune in and really give yourself to learning the voice of God, you will realize that God has been talking to you all the time.

He is never *not* talking or communicating in some way to us. I find that if we have not developed a healthy relationship with an earthly father or mentor, we will oftentimes not feel worthy to hear from God either.

My writing partner Kierra McKenzie is one of the most Prophetic people I have ever met. Our synchronicity is unlike anything I have ever seen or witnessed between two people. We understand 100 percent that it is a Holy Spirit connection, and nothing that we ourselves could orchestrate. Because of how connected we are, God the Father, God the Son or God the Holy Spirit will show up at any time and just begin fellowshipping with us. The presence of God will invade the place we are in, and we will feel Heaven come down to earth. I will describe it as the Kingdom of God, because it doesn't come through observation—it literally is unveiled from inside of us (*Luke 17:20*). And when two or three of us come together in His name, He joins us (*Matthew 18:20*).

When Kierra and I are unfolding a revelation that God has given us, it could come from anywhere: the Word, a vision or a dream. God's primary way to speak to us is through *Rhema* and revelation. There are two words of God, the *logos* (written word of God) and the *Rhema* (right-now spoken word of God.) The *logos* are things that God has said that must be understood within the setting and context. A major crime we as human beings commit is reading things in the Bible out of context, as though everything in it belongs to everyone on the earth. Based on differences in relationship alone, it is not possible for everything in the Bible to correspond to everyone. The Tabernacle itself had three different layers of commitment: the Outer Court, the Inner Court and the Holy of Holies.

So, it makes indisputable Biblical sense that everything in the Bible does not apply to everyone.

Kierra and I will say things that we know came from God, and then the Holy Spirit will pass it back and forward between us until we see what He wants us to see. There are so many times that one of us would totally say what the other was thinking without knowing it. Through this process I have discovered without a shadow of a doubt that God custom-made Kierra and me for this project. Because of Kierra's father issues, she would sometimes doubt if she was hearing the voice of God, even though she prays, intercedes and writes every day through the divine revelation of the Holy Spirit. This book, *Fatherless*, has been written from the inside out. Kierra was having a hard time reconciling her past communication with her father and men in other past relationships. Because of these relationships, she was telling herself that she was not worthy to hear God's voice, or that others could hear Him with better accuracy.

Over time Kierra has become more and more aware of just how powerful her connection to God the Father and His voice is. Now, she can go from earth to Heaven in no time at all, in worship, praise, intercession, prayer, etc. Every day she is becoming more confident in her ability to hear God's voice, and it is because each day she is beginning to see herself the way God the Father sees her and not through the eyes of men. It has been an amazing blessing watching Kierra flourish and seeing her gifting rise day by day as she makes herself available to the Lord.

The Secret Place

You want to know how to hear the voice of God? Become available to Him. You want to cultivate the Prophetic in your life? Practice being quiet and waiting on the Lord. That is one of the biggest and most profound keys in the Bible. Hearing the spiritual voice of God is cultivated in physical silence. There is a tuning and pruning process that happens as you wait on the Lord for prolonged periods of time in complete silence. Yeah, I know it may sound crazy to some, and to others it may prove to be quite difficult, but I promise you that the reward outweighs the sacrifice. There is nothing more Blessed in this world than to hear and discern the voice of God. Once we are born again, it should be the first thing that we learn to do along with developing a hunger and thirst for God's Word.

You can create a Secret Place with God anywhere. In your living room, in your shower, in your closet or in your mind. It's just a place where you and God can be together without interruption or distraction. This is called worship, because at this time you are giving God your full attention. In the Secret Place, God begins to manifest Himself to you. He loves this place, so He desires you to meet Him there regularly. This is called intimacy with God, and as you are intimate with Him, He begins to tell you His secrets, reveal revelations and have Holy Communication with you on a continual basis.

Imagine that some people call Holy Communion the symbolic drinking of wine and eating of bread. This is just a shadow of which daily fellowship in the Garden of Eden with God was a type of. The truth of the matter is that once we are returned to the Father, we have been returned to the Kingdom, and Heaven is literally established wherever this happens, just like in the Garden of Eden (*Genesis 3*).

The Revelator Is the Elevator

Revelations from God lead to high elevations with God. When you see mountains in the Bible, I want you to realize that they are symbolic of levels of revelation with God. When you look at your Bible, you will notice that some of the greatest relationships with God will contain not only the valleys but also some mountaintop experiences. Moses had continual mountaintop experiences with God, and when he brought the people to Mount Sinai, they did not want to have a relationship with God; they wanted Moses to speak to God on their behalf. The revelations that God shares with select sons allowed Moses and Elijah to walk in miracle-working power. It allowed David to walk in New Testament promises while he was still under the Old Covenant. It allowed Jesus to train a group of disciples who would later be filled with the Spirit of God and change the world with the Gospel entrusted to them.

In the last days, the Apostles, Prophets, Evangelists, Pastors and Teachers will come into alignment and walk in the fulness of their power and authority (*Ephesians 4:11-16*). Part of this is revelations that the world has never seen before. In *Acts 2*, Peter is talking to the crowds who think that they are drunk because of the mighty outpouring of the Holy Spirit on the day of Pentecost. Beginning in verse 14 of *Acts 2*, Peter begins to Prophesy:

> *Acts 2:14* — *"But Peter, standing up with the eleven, lifted up his voice, and said unto them, Ye men of Judaea, and all ye that dwell at Jerusalem, be this*

known unto you, and hearken to my words: [15] For these are not drunken, as ye suppose, seeing it is but the third hour of the day. [16] But this is that which was spoken by the prophet Joel; [17] And it shall come to pass in the last days, saith God, I will pour out of my Spirit upon all flesh: and your sons and your daughters shall prophesy, and your young men shall see visions, and your old men shall dream dreams: [18] And on my servants and on my handmaidens I will pour out in those days of my Spirit; and they shall prophesy: [19] And I will shew wonders in heaven above, and signs in the earth beneath; blood, and fire, and vapour of smoke: [20] The sun shall be turned into darkness, and the moon into blood, before the great and notable day of the Lord come: [21] And it shall come to pass, that whosoever shall call on the name of the Lord shall be saved."

God has hidden an amazing revelation in verses 14 to 21, which are not telling of the current outpouring the disciples were experiencing in the upper room of Antioch on the day of Pentecost, but of a time in the future that Joel the Prophet prophesied would happen. It is a revelation and Prophecy of the end-time Revival and harvest of souls that will mark the return of Jesus Christ. This revelation describes God pouring out His spirit upon all flesh.

Baptism of Fire

In the next set of verses, there is a story told by Matthew, Mark and John, but nobody tells the story the way that Matthew does.

Matthew 3:11 — "I indeed baptize you with water unto repentance. but he that cometh after me is mightier than I, whose shoes I am not worthy to bear: he shall baptize you with the Holy Ghost, and with fire: [12] *Whose fan is in his hand, and he will throughly purge his floor, and gather his wheat into the garner; but he will burn up the chaff with unquenchable fire."*

Matthew is describing the story of John the Baptist, who is about to baptize Jesus in the Jordan River. In verse 11, John begins to prophesy and to describe a baptism that will come much later than Jesus' baptism—it will be a baptism of fire. This baptism of fire will purify the Church.

Prayer

Proverbs 3:5 — "Trust in the LORD with all thine heart; and lean not unto thine own understanding. [6] *In all thy ways acknowledge him, and he shall direct thy paths."*

Have you ever been driving somewhere and were sure that you were driving the right way, until you began to see signs that you weren't—and you were lost? Remember that feeling in your stomach and the fear that slowly crept in, whether you were running late or driving in completely unfamiliar territory? This is what it feels like to be lost. What do you do when you're lost? You try to find your way back!

A Christian discovers that he was lost all the time and didn't even know it. We were surrounded by darkness until a Light named Jesus came into our lives and showed us the Way. Now in order to remain in that Way, we have to continue to follow that Light by continuing to be led by His Spirit.

Jesus told the disciples not to leave Jerusalem until they were filled with the Holy Spirit and "endued with power." God literally installed inside of us His navigation system, His GPS ("God Positioning System"). A GPS doesn't give you all 20 directions at the same time; it takes you step by step. No matter what you're doing in the car, no matter what the other cars around you are doing, you have to pay attention to that voice if you want to get to your destination. Do your best to follow every instruction, but it's OK if you make mistakes. The GPS will reroute you to make sure that you reach your destination.

This is what prayer and communication with God looks like. It's not a religious thing; it's a relational thing. It's not out of obligation; it's out of dedication. It's not from the head; it's from the heart. Our communication with God does not originate in a place of legality — it comes from a place of love.

Key Points

1. God began a covenant with Abraham that would be the blueprint for all mankind. *(Genesis 17:1-8)*
2. *The Church's Hierarchy*:
   a. God the Father
   b. God the Son
   c. God the Holy Spirit *(1 John 5:7)*

   The Fivefold Ministry within the Church:
   a. Apostles
   b. Prophets
   c. Evangelists
   d. Teachers
   e. Pastors *(Ephesians 4:11)*

3. God will always ask you for whatever is sitting on the throne of your heart. *(Matthew 19:16-24)*

4. We are always operating in one of two spirits: the Spirit of Adoption or the Orphan Spirit of rebellion. The Orphan Spirit is literally the rebellious spirit of satan. The Spirit of Adoption is the obedient spirit of a son. *(Romans 8:15)*

5. God does not tempt us. We are tempted when we are drawn away by our own lusts. *(James 1:13-15)*

6. God's desire for Israel in the wilderness — and God's desire for the Church right now — is for us to learn to become sons. *(Hebrews 3:6-19)*

7. The doorway to the Kingdom of God is following God with childlike faith. *(Matthew 18:1-4)*

8. True sons of God are led by His Spirit. *(Romans 8:14)*

9. The Holy Spirit is God's GPS. *(Luke 24:49)*

10. There is a Baptism of Fire coming to the Church. *(Matthew 3:11-12)*

Notes

_____

_____

_____

_____

_____

_____

_____

_____

_____

_____

_____

_____

_____

_____

_____

_____

_____

_____

_____

_____

_____

Notes

_____

_____

_____

_____

_____

_____

_____

_____

_____

_____

_____

_____

_____

_____

_____

_____

_____

_____

_____

_____

Notes

_____

_____

_____

_____

_____

_____

_____

_____

_____

_____

_____

_____

_____

_____

_____

_____

_____

_____

_____

_____

_____

_____

_____

_____

CHAPTER 4: DISCIPLESHIP

The Discipline of Discipleship

John 15:8 — "Herein is my Father glorified, that ye bear much fruit; so shall ye be my disciples."

The mark of discipleship is fruitfulness. When the disciples were doing their own thing after Jesus was crucified, He walked up to them while they were fishing and asked them, "Have you any meat?" Now, this was a hypothetical question for them so that Jesus could get them to look at their lives and see what they were doing, to evaluate if they were bearing any fruit, despite their hard labor. Peter was a trained fisherman with a full crew of people, and they had been fishing all night long but still hadn't caught anything *(John 21:5)*. One simple direction from Jesus caused them to catch so many fish that they did not have enough room to carry them all!

Peter thought he knew what he was doing; nevertheless, when he came to the end of himself and let the Master guide him, then he was able to come into a place of supernatural fruitfulness. So, what is God looking for from you? Your "nevertheless"! You may think that you know what to do, but *nevertheless* you put your hand in His hand and let Jesus guide you to abundance that you have never experienced before. This was also to illustrate that once you make it to a certain level of relationship with God, it is no longer about how you did things before but hearing God in the moment for every instruction. Yes, Peter knew how to fish in the physical but the creator of all things was teaching Peter how to navigate in the limitless resources of the spirit by following His voice.

Discipleship demands discipline. The root word of discipleship is *discipline*. Discipline is not something you get overnight. Discipline is doing something over and over and over again. When you're training for anything important, there are some basic things that you practice over and over again until they are instilled in you like muscle memory. Bible reading, prayer, fasting, praise, worship and evangelism are all disciplines that are part of the foundation of being a disciple of Jesus. These are things that you learn to do until they are no longer a duty — they become a part of you. This foundation puts you in a position to learn the greater things of God because you have mastered the basics.

I remember a Sunday morning last year when my pastor was preaching and he quoted someone saying, "Salvation is free, but discipleship will cost you everything." I knew exactly what he meant when he said that. Salvation is a free gift given to us by the Father through His Son, Jesus Christ, and His sacrifice. Discipleship is a process: a little at a time, line upon line, precept upon precept, revelation upon revelation and elevation upon elevation. Each revelation that God gives you as you walk with Him takes you to a new level of elevation up the mountain of relationship. Each revelation that God gives you as you walk with Him zooms your camera lens closer and closer to Jesus and to who He is.

The world is full of churches, and churches are full of Christians, but that fact alone obviously has not brought about a total transformation of the world. The official tally of churches or churchgoers is not what's most important; it is the number of disciples who are living for God that will impact the world. Becoming a Christian only means that you have signed up, but now your commitment is shown by the level of discipleship that you make yourself available for.

How many people sign up for things in order to receive a membership and then never do anything for that organization? How many people have prayed the prayer of salvation and given their lives to the Lord, declaring that God is now Lord of all, and then don't make time for prayer, Bible study, praise, worship and discipleship? I once heard a wise man say, "If He is not Lord of all, He is not Lord at all."

Discipleship is essential to becoming what God has called us to become. There is no such thing as a microwave Christian. The Bible says that our salvation must be walked out with fear and trembling *(Philippians 2:12)*. A father teaches a son step by step as he walks with him through life. This is how God intended for Adam and Eve (and us) to learn. This is a healthy process of growth through relationship.

As you walk with God and encounter new things, you are also learning how to relate to God at the same time. That's why when we get saved, it's called being "born again." Our mistake is when we become born again and pretend that we are already spiritual adults. We then conform to the things that we see the people around us doing, having not yet received the transformation of spiritual maturation.

A Christian without discipleship is **dangerous**. Discipleship allows you to become committed to God by staying in His presence, staying in His Word and staying in communion with Him. This is the real definition of Holy Communion. I promise you that the religious act of drinking grape juice and eating bread will do nothing for you if you are not renewing your mind. When you do it the right way, it's a curse breaker. When you take Holy Communion in the right frame of mind, understanding the meaning of what Jesus did for us, it breaks the curses in our lives and sets in motion the healing that Jesus paid for.

The Design of a Disciple

A disciple is a container. For three and a half years, Jesus was building containers that we call disciples. He said, "You can't put new wine (revelation) into old wineskins (containers)." We are transformed into containers that God can use when we yield to the discipline of the Holy Spirit.

There are a lot of people even in the Body of Christ who think that "discipline" is a curse word. To be honest with you, undeveloped "Christians" still want to do what they want to do, when they want to do it. It's not until we begin living a fasted life that we learn to turn down and deny our flesh. Continually being led and following the promptings of the Holy Spirit is what brings discipline. Giving ourselves to scheduled times of Bible reading, prayer, church and Christian fellowship is what brings discipline.

I will be honest with you: The flesh is not happy with discipline, and it will not surrender without a fight. Discipline requires the exchange of your comfort zone for your spiritual purpose and destiny to be unfolded. Discipline required Cain to follow the full instructions that God had given him. Rebellion says, "Naaaaah, I can do it how I want to do it, and God will be happy with it. He should just be happy that I made a sacrifice anyway." But the Bible says that it's not the *sacrifice* that God is impressed with but the *obedience* in following His instructions.

How can God put us in charge of angels and planets in the future if we can't follow the smallest instructions on earth? The higher we go up the mountain of relationship with God, it requires more discipline. It's nothing to worry or be stressed about — because in the end we can't do anything without the Holy Spirit. You might be saying to yourself, "Lord knows I tried to be disciplined in my Bible reading and prayer time, but it's just so hard." Holy Spirit helps us do any and everything that we need to do. But how much access we give Him will determine the speed of our development.

God cannot put inside of you what you cannot contain. As much as you may want it, God wants it even more than you do. God gives all of us a calling, and an anointing to fulfill that calling, but most of our life is spent with God preparing the container for what He has called us to do.

Have you ever seen greatness in a bad container? A person who was gifted and world renowned for their gifts and talents but possessed terrible character and personality? There are people who have fame, fortune and influence, and instead of using it for positivity to lift people up to a higher level of consciousness and achievement, they bring people down into depravity and destruction. Some people in our society actually are systematically lifted up so that they can lead a large majority of people to destruction. There are people who take advantage of the condition of fatherlessness to destroy generation after generation of certain people groups. Money and media airtime are thrown into promoting debauchery in order to influence and program young minds. It literally only takes one song, one idea or one movement to lead people to destruction.

When God created us in His image *(Genesis 1:27)*, His purpose was to make a vessel that was exactly like Him. God's intent for mankind was to make us gods (with a little "g"). God is sovereign (the only One with a big "G"), and He rules and reigns. His desire and purpose for mankind is to raise up sons and daughters who He can trust to rule and reign the galaxies with Him.

Be Still

Whatever we have been called to, we have to be present in. This is called discipline. You can't be a member of five different churches, because what happens is that every time things get hard, you hop to a new place and you never get changed. Staying in one place — in one relationship, in one family and in one church — challenges us to change.

There are some things that you will never see inside of you until you are in a relationship that reveals them and shines the light of consciousness on them. For example, you never know you are a jealous person until you get into a relationship and jealousy exposes itself. You never know you have anger issues until you are in situations that cause anger to expose itself. There are things inside of us that hide until they are exposed through relationship.

Going around from place to place does not allow opportunities for deep, meaningful relationships; therefore, you will never get to the deep, hidden things inside of you. Just about anyone can look perfect for a few days, but when you begin to spend time with someone and the guard drops, then what's inside of you begins to reveal itself. All the occupants of your soul don't show themselves all at once. As you walk alongside someone, they find the opportunity to be seen. This is why we must be pastored, we must be discipled and we must have accountability partners.

> *Proverbs 11:14 — "Where no counsel is, the people fall: but in the multitude of counsellors there is safety."*

We are reminding those brothers and sisters who do not have solid church homes, relationships and healthy church congregations to sit still, get grounded and rooted, and let God work things out in them using the tool called *relationship*.

Picture a relationship as you and another person in a boat together. The communication that goes back and forth is called a "*relay*-tionship." Both people in the relationship have to row the boat. Now, suppose one person keeps jumping in and out of the boat. The boat will become unstable, stagnate and take much longer to reach its location than it could have if both parties participated. We need to be pruned, fertilized and cultivated through relationships. This is called community, this is called family and this is called stability that you find in being discipled. We don't get anywhere by ourselves. God puts people around us to help us become what we were created to be.

The Church

Discipleship is **not** an option. It is essential. And we are called the Body of Christ — not "the body part of Christ on a solo mission to save the world." Family forces us to grow. Family forces us to stretch. And family forces us to learn how to love.

When I hear people praying for revival, it makes something inside of me cringe. Because I look around and see a group of people who are not loving the 20 or so people around them in the room, but yet we are praying for revival. Should God send us a thousand more people to ignore, be bitter against, backbite and be offended by? We believe that if we learn how to love the people that God has given us in our community, with one mind and one accord in agreement, then God can add to the church daily as many as will be saved.

The cross is a horizontal and a vertical love working together in unison. Family is essential for helping us understand the mystery of the cross.

Every person is a body part and a member of the Body of Christ. Every piece complements the Body. We have similarities, but we are not the same. We are different, but we are all one. All of the body parts are doing different things, but they are all working together for your good at the same time. This is the beauty of the Body of Christ.

1 Corinthians 12:12 — "For as the body is one, and hath many members, and all the members of that one body, being many, are one body: so also is Christ. [13] For by one Spirit are we all baptized into one body, whether we be Jews or Gentiles, whether we be bond or free; and have been all made to drink into one Spirit. [14] For the body is not one member, but many."

So, look around at your brothers and sisters and appreciate them... Appreciate their diversity, their uniqueness, their attributes, the things that set them apart. Sometimes we want people to be exactly the way we are, but that expectation is not realistic. Each person has his or her own job, anointing and administrations.

Listen

The ability to listen is an amazing trait. These days, it seems like it's harder than ever before to get people to listen. In our YouTube generation of learners, the attention span of most people is much shorter than it ever was in the past. Distractions are all around us, fighting for our attention 24 hours a day. We hold a device in our hand called a cell phone that is constantly giving us notifications for umpteen different apps working at the same time. Our cell phones have literally become a distraction device.

Have you ever tried to tell something to someone who just wouldn't listen? I mean, you had something really important to tell them, but, in their mind, they felt that what they had to say was more important. How can a father teach a son who will not listen? How could God pour everything into Jesus that He wanted to pour into Him if He wouldn't listen? Jesus was the model for the perfect son.

I know this may seem basic and trivial, but it's not. In order to get a person to listen to you, you have to get them to sit down, give you their attention and allow you to hold that attention for the duration of what you want to say. This in itself requires a lot of discipline from your listener.

Distraction

We have only begun to see the effects of technology and social media on our world today. The human race is becoming less sensitive to their environment and the people around them. Once a person plugs into their devices, they become like robots, and it's difficult to get their attention. You see people running into walls, walking hazardously in the street, causing deadly accidents — all because of this addiction to their devices. If people are constantly feeding their minds with violence, murder, perversion, unrealistic fantasies and negative news, then it is easy to witness someone else getting raped, stabbed or hit by a car and it not phase them because they've already seen it over and over again. They no longer value human life. This has become the reality of our world.

Our challenge in this current generation is to raise up disciples in the midst of a multitude of distractions. There are more TV channels, shows, apps, devices and ways to be distracted than ever before in the history of mankind. What should you give your attention to? Well, that depends on your purpose, your identity and your destiny. What do you want to be? What path are you on? And what steps are you taking to get to your destination?

Are you distracted? How would you know? How hard is it for you to focus? Well, here's a little test to help you self-evaluate just how distracted you may be:

1. How many apps do you have on your phone?
2. How much time do you spend on your phone each day?
3. How much time do you spend playing games?
4. How much time do you spend on social media?

5. How much time do you spend in front of technological devices?
6. How much time do you spend sleeping?
7. How much time do you lose in fruitless conversations?
8. How much time do you spend eating?
9. How many hours do you spend shopping?

Everything we mentioned above are time-stealers. Things that seem little can quickly add up to lost hours, days, weeks, months and years. I mean, just the average person who sleeps eight hours per day actually spends one-third of their life sleeping. Imagine how much time distractions, when added up, take out of our lives? One of the biggest problems in our current culture could probably be called distraction.

Distraction is so subtle: It just wants a little bit of your time... Two hours later, a chunk of your day is gone. *Hmmm... This little game right here is a lot of fun. I mean, I deserve a little stress release.* Before you know it, we are addicted to the dopamine released by stacking up colored candy or shooting enemies on the battlefield of our favorite game. None of these things mentioned above is wrong or a sin, but the point is to recognize destiny-stealers before they steal our time, money and moments with others away. Let's all be more mindful of avoiding distractions.

Seedtime and Harvest

Genesis 8:22 — "While the earth remaineth, seedtime and harvest, and cold and heat, and summer and winter, and day and night shall not cease."

In the field of our soul, there are things that every person must deal with. The Bible says that there are tares sown among the wheat. It's like that for the Body of Christ and also for us as individuals. We are all born in sin and shaped in iniquity; therefore, we are already born with some generational curses that need to be dealt with. In addition to that, we have doors that we have knowingly and unknowingly opened to the spirit realm.

Our soul is a field and we, as the farmers, are responsible for the management of that field. Some of our fields look like junkyards; some of our fields are covered in weeds and debris. No matter the condition of our field, we ALL have some things in our field that need to be uprooted. If we ignore the weeds that are present in our field, they will eventually grow into fruition.

Perfection

Growing up, I remember a game called Perfection. In this game, there is a platform that has shapes cut out of it, like stars, circles, rectangles and several other shapes. The object of the game is to start the timer, press down the platform and get all the pieces in place before the time runs out. The player has to grab one piece at a time and figure out which place it fits into. If you finish putting the pieces in place before the timer goes off, you win the game. If you don't place every piece in time, the platform suddenly pops up and — *bang* — the pieces go flying everywhere.

I have always seen that game as an analogy in the spirit as I have walked with God. The timer is ticking right now for all of us, and we are all in a race toward perfection. Some people say, "Nobody is perfect," but I don't believe that.

Matthew 5:48 — "Be ye therefore perfect, even as your Father which is in heaven is perfect."

James 1:4 — "But let patience have her perfect work, that ye may be perfect and entire, wanting nothing."

As we walk with God, we must know that level after level of amazing breakthroughs are available to us. Why should we seek after higher levels in God? Well, the answer to that question is simple. There are many people in this world who need God and everything that Jesus presented to us from the Kingdom of God in *Luke 4:18-19*:

"The Spirit of the Lord is upon me, because he hath anointed me to preach the gospel to the poor; he hath sent me to heal the brokenhearted, to preach deliverance to the captives, and recovering of sight to the blind, to set at liberty them that are bruised, to preach the acceptable year of the Lord."

As we mentioned before, the Spirit of the Lord came upon Jesus for service. God was very intentional about the mission that He had for Jesus, as Jesus was doing only those things that He saw the Father do. So, what was Jesus doing exactly? He was promoting the Kingdom of God by walking in the "Christ" — the Anointed One and His anointing.

Luke 4:18-19
1. Preach the Gospel to the poor.
2. Heal the brokenhearted.
3. Preach deliverance to the captives.
4. Recovery of sight to the blind
5. Set at Liberty those that were bruised.
6. Preach the acceptable year of the Lord.

What is Perfection, you might ask? Perfection is wholeheartedly giving your life to God, surrendering to the Holy Spirit and walking in the identity, purpose and destiny that He has created you for. Perfection is not instantaneous; it is a high-bar and goal that we run toward. *Philippians 3:14* says, *"I press toward the mark for the prize of the high calling of God in Christ Jesus."* In my opinion, we can reach Perfection by being intentional about these things:

1. Learning His voice, obeying and following the Holy Spirit.
2. Being available to Holy Spirit for daily prayer and communion.
3. Having and cultivating a hunger and thirst for the Word and things of God.
4. Having and cultivating an appetite for Praise, Worship and True Intimacy with God.
5. Walking in Humility.
6. Walking in Honor.
7. Regular church attendance and fellowship.
8. Joining a cell discipleship group.

Salvation is a relationship that needs to be intentionally managed as we walk with Jesus toward Perfection. *Ephesians 4:11-13* not only says that we can and should be perfect, but it highlights the people in the Body of Christ who are chosen and anointed by God to help us reach perfection:

"And he gave some, apostles; and some, prophets; and some, evangelists; and some, pastors and teachers; [12] *For the perfecting of the saints, for the work of the ministry, for the edifying of the body of Christ:* [13] *Till we all come in the unity of the faith, and of the knowledge*

of the Son of God, unto a <u>perfect man</u>, unto the measure of the stature of the fulness of Christ."

Humans have made up many spiritual systems, theologies, denominations and organizations, but the true hierarchy has only three pieces: Father, Son and Holy Spirit. After the Godhead, the Bible goes on in *Ephesians 4:14-16* to elaborate on the job, authority and importance of the five-fold ministry:

"That we henceforth be no more children, tossed to and fro, and carried about with every wind of doctrine, by the sleight of men, and cunning craftiness, whereby they lie in wait to deceive; [15] But speaking the truth in love, may grow up into him in all things, which is the head, even Christ: [16] From whom the whole body fitly joined together and compacted by that which every joint supplieth, according to the effectual working in the measure of every part, maketh increase of the body unto the edifying of itself in love."

Key Points

1. The mark of discipleship is fruitfulness. *(Galatians 5:22-23)*
2. Discipleship demands discipline. The root word for discipleship is "discipline." *(Matthew 13:10)*
3. We are all a body part that is connected to a body. We must honor every body part and work together in unity

for the body to be effective. *(1 Corinthians 12:12-14)*

4. Our soul is a field and we, as the farmers, are responsible for the management of that field. If we ignore the weeds that are present in our field, they will eventually grow into fruition. *(Genesis 8:22)*

5. We must allow God to be made perfect in us so that we can do those things that Jesus did and greater. The world needs the Kingdom of God that we as sons embody. *(James 1:4, Luke 4:18-19)*

Notes

Notes

Notes

_____

_____

_____

_____

_____

_____

_____

_____

_____

_____

_____

_____

_____

_____

_____

_____

_____

_____

_____

_____

_____

_____

FATHERLESS

CHAPTER 5: HONOR

Chief Master Builder/Apostle

Psalm 127:1 — *"Except the LORD build the house, they labour in vain that build it: except the LORD keep the city, the watchman waketh but in vain."*

When the Apostles and Prophets were taken out of the house of God, the eyes and the blueprints were taken away from the Church. The fathers and the seers were taken out of the Body of Christ. The Prophets are the eyes, ears and seers of God, and the Apostles download and dictate the blueprint of God. They are the fathers, who carry the Father's heart and ensure that discipline is established in the Church. Without discipline, we contend for the faith because we can neither keep nor contain it. Discipline is what allows us to hold on to what God gives us. This is why Jesus started with disciples. The Apostle and the Prophet working together are an unstoppable team.

The Apostle Paul, in *1 Corinthians 13:9-10*, says, *"For we know in part, and we prophesy in part. But when that which is perfect is come, then that which is in part shall be done away."* Any pieces of knowledge that we have are just parts. When you get rid of the Apostles and the Prophets, you have no way to build what God wants to build, because these are the people who God downloads the blueprints to. Without the Apostle and the Prophet, all you have are pieces to have church with, and you could never have "that which is perfect."

Whenever God builds something — whether it's the Ark of the Covenant, the Temple of David, Noah's Ark or the Tabernacle — it is always built with exact specifications. The Bible calls the Apostles the fathers of the church, and this is one of the reasons why *Malachi 4:6* says that there must be a restoration of the hearts of the fathers to the sons, and the hearts of the sons to the fathers. Without the Apostles there are no fathers, and without the fathers there are no sons whose manifestation all of creation is groaning and waiting for (*Romans 8:19*).

1 Corinthians 4:9 — *"For I think that God hath set forth us the apostles last, as it were appointed to death: for we are made a spectacle unto the world, and to angels, and to men. [10] We are fools for Christ's sake, but ye are wise in Christ; we are weak, but ye are strong; ye are honourable, but we are despised. [11] Even unto this present hour we both hunger, and thirst, and are naked, and are buffeted, and have no certain dwellingplace; [12] And labour, working with our own hands: being reviled, we bless; being persecuted, we suffer it: [13] Being defamed, we intreat: we are made as the filth of the world, and are the offscouring of all things unto this day. [14] I write not these things to shame you, but as my beloved sons I warn you. [15] For though ye have ten thousand instructers in Christ, yet have ye not many fathers: for in Christ Jesus I have begotten you through the gospel."*

With all the words that God has given you — the revelations, the blessings, the answered prayers that God has given you — why aren't you moving into the things that God has called you to? What is behind your paralysis? Why don't certain pieces of your life ever come together? What is out of alignment? I believe that the answer to these questions is that God has given us many pieces, but it is a father of the faith who shows us where the pieces go. The Bible calls the Apostle Paul "a wise master builder":

1 Corinthians 3:10 — "According to the grace of God which is given unto me, as a wise masterbuilder, I have laid the foundation, and another buildeth thereon. But let every man take heed how he buildeth thereupon."

This means that people and pieces can be anointed, but it is the appointment from God that is understood and followed by the Apostle-led church. Many houses of God are being built, but how many of those are following the fivefold ministry blueprint of God? I truly believe that we are coming into a season where there will be a huge difference between the churches that are following God's blueprint and those that are following the blueprint of a person, organization or denomination. Anything that is not Spirit-led is going to be as dry as the desert, and you're going to know the trees by the fruit that they bear.

God is about to unveil a glorious Church that is without spot or wrinkle, and it will be birthed out of the Spirit of God, along with those who are willing to build God's house according to His specifications. Pastors will be given the choice to give God what He's asking for and be blessed, or to do things their own way and be unavailable for the Glory of God.

Spiritual Chiropractic Alignment

> *2 Chronicles 16:9 — "For the eyes of the LORD run to and fro throughout the whole earth, to shew himself strong in the behalf of them whose heart is perfect toward him. Herein thou hast done foolishly: therefore from henceforth thou shalt have wars."*

Right now, God's eyes are going to and fro in the earth, looking for a Church that will walk in unity, holiness and obedience. We see in *1 Corinthians 14:40* that "Everything must be done decently and in order," and God does have an order. Not only does God have an order, but He also has a Chain-of-Command that we just outlined in *Ephesians 4:11*. In the end times, God will build His Church upon the blueprint and Chain-of-Command led by His Apostles. *Malachi 4:6* will come into fruition as the true fathers return to the sons and the sons return to the fathers. We call this "Spiritual Chiropractic Alignment." This type of alignment will position the Church to walk in a way that is pleasing to Father God — and therefore present a bride to Him for our Savior Jesus —a glorious Church that is without spot or wrinkle.

> *Ephesians 5:27— "That he might present it to himself a glorious church, not having spot, or wrinkle, or any such thing; but that it should be holy and without blemish."*

Honor

Honor: "one whose worth brings respect."[8]

Honor is incredibly important. We are supposed to learn and establish our grid for honor as we look at our mother and father. If we learned to honor properly in our relationship with our parents, we would now have the basis to honor others outside of our family. If we neglect to honor our mother and father, it then becomes so easy not to honor authorities, teachers, police officers, government officials and every other relationship in our life.

Honor, like love, begins with honoring and loving yourself, for only then are you able to honor and love others *(Mark 12:30-31)*. Love and honor exist side by side. The Bible commands us to love our neighbor as we love ourselves. You can't truly love someone without honoring them.

Honor must be both horizontal and vertical. It is not possible for us to say that we honor God vertically if we don't honor our brothers and sisters horizontally. This is what the cross looks like. The cross is a union of a vertical relationship with God that allows us to have a horizontal relationship with the world around us. We as sons of God are literally bringing Heaven down to earth. We become God's translators of what Kingdom culture and family are supposed to look like. We can't crawl over, knock down, run over and step on people to get to God.

> *1 John 4:20 — "If a man say, I love God, and hateth his brother, he is a liar: for he that loveth not his brother whom he hath seen, how can he love God whom he hath not seen? [21] And this commandment have we from him, That he who loveth God love his brother also."*

> *Mark 12:30 (NIV) — "Love the Lord your God with all your heart and with all your soul and with all your mind and with all your strength. [31] The second is this:*

'Love your neighbor as yourself.' There is no commandment greater than these."

You can't use the invisible God as an excuse not to take care of the visible people who are around you. Everything we do must be Spirit led. Anything that is truly Spirit led will complement you and be an asset to your life.

The devil comes to steal, kill and destroy, and he will use religion as a tool to do that. The devil often hides behind religious ideas and agendas, stealing the very life out of the people, because what's being done is motivated by the flesh instead of the Holy Spirit. If the devil cannot stop us from moving forward, he will sometimes get behind us and push us off balance. If whatever spiritual activities we are participating in — like prayer, fasting, praise, worship and offerings — are not life giving, then they are probably energy stealing. The right thing can very easily become the wrong thing, when the motive is not Kingdom and we are not being led by Holy Spirit. Learning to operate in God's timing, with His voice and with the motivation of building His Kingdom in love is essential.

Honor in the Church

No matter what you think about the different parts of your body, you must honor, take care of and respect each one. Each part must be washed and attended to, and if you neglect any part of your body, it won't be long until that neglect is openly noticeable to yourself and to the public. An arm must be respected as an arm, and it must be allowed to carry out arm duties. You can't let your ego get in the way and start treating an arm like a leg. Your arm might be able to do some of the same things that a leg does for a while, but it wasn't built for that purpose.

When you are a leader in the Body of Christ, you must be super-sensitive about honoring the members of the Body that God sends into your congregation. When we talk about "rightly discerning the Body of Christ," we often focus on Holy Communion without considering that the Body of Christ is a group of people and a family. We must honor each body part, for by doing so we receive the reward that comes from extending honor. I have heard from the Holy Spirit and personally believe that the answers to our problems, healing and ministry that we need are most often right among our brothers and sisters in the church, cell group or prayer team.

> *1 Corinthians 11:29* — *"For he that eateth and drinketh unworthily, eateth and drinketh damnation to himself, not discerning the Lord's body."*

> *Matthew 10:41* — *"He that receiveth a prophet in the name of a prophet shall receive a prophet's reward; and he that receiveth a righteous man in the name of a righteous man shall receive a righteous man's reward."*

The Revelation of the Five Pools of Bethesda

> *John 5:1* — *"After this there was a feast of the Jews; and Jesus went up to Jerusalem. ² Now there is at Jerusalem by the sheep market a pool, which is called in the Hebrew tongue Bethesda, having five porches. ³ In these lay a great multitude of impotent folk, of blind, halt, withered, waiting for the moving of the water. ⁴ For an angel went down at a certain season into the pool, and troubled the water: whosoever then first after the troubling of the water stepped in was made whole of whatsoever disease he had. ⁵ And a certain man was there, which had an infirmity thirty and eight years. ⁶ When Jesus saw him lie, and knew that he had*

been now a long time in that case, he saith unto him, Wilt thou be made whole? [7] The impotent man answered him, Sir, I have no man, when the water is troubled, to put me into the pool: but while I am coming, another steppeth down before me. [8] Jesus saith unto him, Rise, take up thy bed, and walk."

The Holy Spirit revealed to me that the five pools of Bethesda in *John 5* are a revelation of people who were hurt and misused by the Church. Here's a brief explanation of the correlation: John 5, fivefold ministries, five pools of Bethesda. So many people have been hurt by the Church because they were dishonored. Their gifting, their talents and their callings were not recognized and cultivated by the church leader over them in the position of authority. When a father does not recognize your gifts and your talents, it opens the door of opportunity for spirits of rebellion, resentment, rejection, low self-esteem, low self-image and every other spirit under the umbrella of the Orphan Spirit. Many of these people are still crippled and waiting for the season where God raises up His Church and returns the heart of the Father to its members. Fathers will raise up sons, and sons will bring the lost to the Father.

Kingdom Vitamins

There are some moments or seasons when God separates us to be alone with Him, and there are some levels in God that cannot be achieved by yourself. When you are alone, the Father is perfecting one particular member of the Body, and when we are working together, He is perfecting the Body as a whole. There are some vitamins that we can only get from each other:

> ➢ Vitamin F_1 = Family

- ➢ Vitamin F_2 = Father
- ➢ Vitamin M = Mother
- ➢ Vitamin B = Brother
- ➢ Vitamin S = Sister
- ➢ Vitamin L = Love

There are some vitamins that are necessary for the healing, cultivation and fertilization of our souls. We believe that some mental problems are caused by these vitamin deficiencies. God is able to give you any vitamin that you need through any person who is willing to be His conduit. This means that you may not be a father, but He can give the Father's love through you if you know the Father. Just like a postman delivering a letter for the post office, anyone working for the postal system who is qualified to deliver mail can give you your mail. And a person who knows the Father's love can become like the "I AM" and become any vitamin He needs you to be for someone in that moment.

Honor in Parenting

People often have children without honoring their children or the position of being a parent. Being a parent is a position of honor that God has entrusted to you. God is trusting you to nurture and raise an eternal being for His purpose. You are raising a human being with tremendous meaning. You are a portal bringing a human being into this earth, a child who has a purpose, a destiny and an identity.

You have to give your children their identity, which is an ID card that they will carry around for the rest of their life. Now, no matter what they encounter, your children will know that they have a purpose and a reason that they were created for.

Every human being was born to answer a question (or questions) that the earth is asking. People in times past used to know the name and the purpose of their children before they were even born. Abraham received the names and the destinies of his children directly from God the Father. So, now when Abraham looked into Isaac's eyes, and later when Isaac looked into Jacob's eyes, the fathers knew exactly what needed to be passed down.

Elevation (Promotion Time)

Kingdom Graduation Ceremony on the Mount of Transfiguration

Read this next set of verses very carefully as we unravel a mystery that has been sitting right in front of our eyes ever since the formation of the New Testament. Why did God the Father show up twice in Jesus' time on earth, making what seemed to be the same statement? Examine the verses below and realize that He didn't say the same thing twice. What happened on the mountain of transfiguration is one of the greatest mysteries in the Bible, and this is what happened:

> *Matthew 17:1 (NIV) — "After six days Jesus took with him Peter, James and John the brother of James, and led them up a high mountain by themselves. ² There he was transfigured before them. His face shone like the sun, and his clothes became as white as the light. ³ Just then there appeared before them Moses and Elijah, talking with Jesus. ⁴ Peter said to Jesus, 'Lord, it is good for us to be here. If you wish, I will put up three shelters—one for you, one for Moses and one for Elijah.' ⁵ While he was still speaking, a bright cloud covered them, and a voice from the cloud said, 'This is my Son,*

whom I love; with him I am well pleased. Listen to him!'
*[6] When the disciples heard this, they fell facedown to
the ground, terrified. [7] But Jesus came and touched
them. 'Get up,' he said. 'Don't be afraid.' [8] When they
looked up, they saw no one except Jesus. [9] As they were
coming down the mountain, Jesus instructed them,
'Don't tell anyone what you have seen, until the Son of
Man has been raised from the dead.' [10] The disciples
asked him, 'Why then do the teachers of the law say
that Elijah must come first?' [11] Jesus replied, 'To be
sure, Elijah comes and will restore all things. [12] But I
tell you, Elijah has already come, and they did not
recognize him, but have done to him everything they
wished. In the same way the Son of Man is going to
suffer at their hands.' [13] Then the disciples understood
that he was talking to them about John the Baptist."*

The beginning of *Matthew 17* contains an incredible
account of Jesus' Kingdom Sonship confirmation service.
We often assume that Jesus came to earth in the power of
His full Godliness. This is not the case, because if it were,
He couldn't show us the way. He had to show us a way that
we could duplicate, meaning He had to strip down and take
off His Godly form in order to become a man. Then He
had to walk out His relationship with God the Father, step
by step, just like any man would have to do.

After you understand this, you will better understand
the two times that God the Father said, "This is my beloved
Son." The first time that God says, "This is my beloved
Son," in *Matthew 3:17*, Jesus is being filled with the Holy
Spirit as He comes down upon Jesus as a dove. Once we
are filled with the Spirit, it is then the job of the Holy Spirit
to clean us up and make us sons.

The second time that the Father says, *"This is my
beloved Son, in whom I am well pleased; hear ye Him,"*

is in *Matthew 17:5*. The first time that He said it, Jesus was given the baptism of the Holy Spirit; the second time that He said it, Jesus was given a confirmation of power and authority as the Son of God. In other words, Jesus walked with God until God Himself confirmed His Sonship with signs and wonders following. *Ahhhhh!* Now you see why the world is full of churches and "Christians" but not with signs and wonders. Because *Romans 8* says that "creation is groaning, waiting for sons to be manifested." What allows the Holy Spirit to change the **called** "children of God" into **chosen** "sons of God"? *Romans 8:19-23* points to the act of being adopted:

> *Romans 8:19 (AMP)* — *"For [even the whole] creation [all nature] waits eagerly for the children of God to be revealed. ²⁰ For the creation was subjected to frustration and futility, not willingly [because of some intentional fault on its part], but by the will of Him who subjected it, in hope ²¹ that the creation itself will also be freed from its bondage to decay [and gain entrance] into the glorious freedom of the children of God. ²² For we know that the whole creation has been moaning together as in the pains of childbirth until now. ²³ And not only this, but we too, who have the first fruits of the Spirit [a joyful indication of the blessings to come], even we groan inwardly, as we wait eagerly for [the sign of] our adoption as sons—the redemption and transformation of our body [at the resurrection]."*

As you read *Matthew 17*, notice that Jesus takes His top three disciples up to a high mountain. Jesus prayed to God every day on a high mountain, but in this particular case He decided to take Peter, James and John with Him. At this elevation, Jesus' intent was to give those disciples a new revelation. The mountain is symbolic of relationship with God. The wide bottom represents the outer court, where anyone can go. As you ascend, you reach the inner court, where only the **called** ascend to. But as you keep climbing to the top of the mountain, you get to the Holy of Holies, where only the **chosen** can enter.

People like to say that God is not a respecter of persons, and He is not. He is a respecter of principles. And one of those principles is "If you draw near to God, He will draw near to you" (*James 4:8*). I heard a great man of God say something that has stuck with me until this very day: "You are as close to God right now as you want to be." When I heard this statement, it excited me because it let me know that I have the option to get as close to God as I am willing to invest the time.

It's really time for us to stop assuming that everything in the Bible applies to every person. IT DOES NOT! The Bible is a book of relationship, and every story is based on a relationship between God and man. Everyone did not walk on water, everyone did not multiply food and everyone did not heal the sick and raise the dead, even though they probably wanted to.

This is the same reason why people don't do the things that Jesus did in the Bible — because they have not followed His example. If we ever as a Church expect to do what Jesus did "and greater," we must follow His pattern. This means following the path of Salvation that Jesus outlined until our sonship is confirmed and manifested.

What does a world filled with the sons of God look like?

The Kingdom of God

During our study and mediation time, the Holy Spirit revealed to us that the number 17 is the number of Kingdom. Everything is marked, and signs ALWAYS follow them that believe *(Mark:16:17)*. So, now when you read the Bible, pay attention, and you will see the fingerprints of the Kingdom of God, wherever you see 17. In Matthew 17:1 - We see the revelation and merging together of denominations to create one Kingdom family. There is a ceremony happening that ONLY Peter, James, and John were invited to attend with Jesus. At this ceremony, Moses and Elijah showed up to talk with Jesus as they were illuminated together. Their clothing changed as they came together under one Kingdom mantle.

Peter, then says he wants to build three tents, symbolic of three denominations, but God said, "This is my beloved Son in whom I am well pleased, hear Ye Him." This was the unification of three different dispensations under one Kingdom rule. Jesus, the King of Kings was now unifying three of the most powerful ministries that the world had ever seen. The new order of things will not just be the Old Testament or just the New Testament, but the Kingdom Testament.

This experience was the prophetic precursor to the season that we are now in. A season where we all come together as one, lay our individual accomplishments down, and enter into unity as the sons of God; representatives of the Kingdom of Heaven. This will not be a popular message for everyone, because it will require people to lay down their denominations and be Kingdom; God's family. This is a necessary step in order for us to become illuminated and transfigured by God, into the sons of God that creation is groaning and waiting for *(Romans 8:19)*.

Key Points

1. The Prophets are the eyes, ears and seers of God, and the Apostles download and dictate the blueprint of God. They are the fathers, who carry the Father's heart and ensure that discipline is established in the church. *(Ephesians 4:11-13)*
2. Honor must be horizontal and vertical. *(1 John 4:20)*
3. The five pools of Bethesda in John 5 are a revelation of people who were hurt and misused by the Church. A brief explanation of the correlation: John 5, fivefold ministries, five pools of Bethesda. *(John 5:1-8)*
4. Honor your children by knowing their destiny beforehand (receiving their ID card from God) and by speaking their proper God-given identity into them. *(Genesis 49:22-28)*
5. The Kingdom Graduation Ceremony on the Mount of Transfiguration is the graduation ceremony of the sons of God. *(Matthew 17:1-13)*
6. The death of denominations. All denominations that carry the same theological truths of the Father, Son and Holy Spirit, should merge into one kingdom family. Denominations keep us divided. *(Matthew 17)*

Notes

_____

_____

_____

_____

_____

_____

_____

_____

_____

_____

_____

_____

_____

_____

_____

_____

_____

_____

_____

_____

_____

Notes

_____

_____

_____

_____

_____

_____

_____

_____

_____

_____

_____

_____

_____

_____

_____

_____

_____

_____

_____

_____

Notes

_____
_____
_____
_____
_____
_____
_____
_____
_____
_____
_____
_____
_____
_____
_____
_____
_____
_____
_____
_____
_____
_____
_____

CHAPTER 6: REDEMPTION, RESTORATION AND RECONCILIATION

Jesus, the Reverse of Every Curse

The Holy Spirit showed us something interesting: We noticed that things representing the devil tend to start with the letters "de-" while things representing Jesus start with "Re-". For example, the devil is linked to the words deceiver, deception, depravity and destruction. Jesus, on the other hand, is the R.E.: the Redeemer, Restorer, Resurrection, Reconciliation, etc. Jesus is the Reverse of Every Curse. Every evil intention of satan already has a remedy provided in Jesus. *John 10:10* says;

> *"The thief cometh not, but for to steal, and to kill, and to destroy: I am come that they might have life, and that they might have it more abundantly."*

Jesus became a curse for us, being hung on a tree, which then allowed Him to become the antidote for every curse that could ever come upon mankind.

So, what we are saying to you is that the medicine is always ready in Jesus, and all we have to do is apply it by being in correct covenant and agreement with God's Word. Curses are word-covenant agreements that we open ourselves up to in conversations, songs, declarations and so on. This is what the Bible means when it says, *"Life and death are in the power of the tongue" (Proverbs 18:21)*. We have the power to speak blessings of life or curses of death into people's lives with our words. Our words are so important that the Bible says that we will be judged by every word that comes out of our mouths.

> *Matthew 12:35 — "A good man out of the good treasure of the heart bringeth forth good things: and an evil man out of the evil treasure bringeth forth evil things. But I say unto you, That every idle word that men shall speak, they shall give account thereof in the day of judgment. For by thy words thou shalt be justified, and by thy words thou shalt be condemned."*

The Spirit and Curse of Rebellion

Ever since the moment that Adam and Eve sinned, they were cursed (empowered to fail) and started walking in the Spirit of Rebellion. Rebellion qualifies you for every curse that falls upon the children of disobedience, just as obedience to God, conversely, qualifies you for every blessing.

As a young person, I was filled with pride, jealousy, envy, perversion, stubbornness, selfishness, lust and all manner of evil because of the rebellion in my heart against my earthly father. Because according to my heart I had not received from him what I believe I should have received as a daughter, therefore I would not give him what he desired to receive from me as his child. When he spoke to me from the pools of wisdom inside of him, my heart was closed, and by closing my heart to him, I opened my heart up to satan in the same way that Adam did when he disobeyed God the Father.

The adversary was able to trick Eve by making her think that God was holding something back from her, but the truth was that He had already freely given her everything. Rebellion is based on a false perception of us not receiving something that we think we should have. We literally make a partnership with a lie and therefore open up a door for more lies to come into our heart. Then we live a life of lies, looking through the filter of our false perception of what we did not get from our parents. This becomes our prescription, and every relationship is seen through this prescription and tainted until we get healed.

Now think about that: How many relationships have you messed up based on what you thought you were not receiving from the other person? When, in reality, it was not the other person's fault; it was the broken little girl or boy inside of you telling you what you did not receive, over and over like an echo in your soul.

Temptation

We have to be aware of what seats are available inside of our soul if we truly want to be pure before God. People who walk in an Orphan Spirit have a lot of seats in their heart for the devil to sit on. The enemy has no place in your heart unless you have a seat that is open for him to use. When the devil saw Saul's jealousy toward David, he found a way in and built his habitation inside of Saul's heart. The devil can only get in your heart if there is a seat available for him. But if you decide to be offense-proof, where can he sit?

Jesus was the One who said, "He has no place in me" *(John 14:30)*. The devil came to Jesus after His time of fasting and was searching in Jesus for a place where he could sit down. The lust of the flesh, the lust of the eyes and the pride of life are the three categories of temptation that satan first tempted Jesus with, and therefore he tries to tempt all of mankind with these same things *(1 John 2:16)*.

You always hear about the devil buying people's souls, but I want to assert that the devil can't buy your soul if it's not for sale! If you decide to be offense-proof, the devil has no place to sit in your heart against you or someone else. To clarify that a little more: If we are allowing love to "cover a multitude of faults" *(1 Peter 4:8)*, people in our lives will do wrong things to us knowingly or unknowingly, but our love will be so thick that their actions won't really matter as much because staying in God's love is more important to us. "Bearing all things, believing all things, hoping all things and enduring all things" *(1 Corinthians 13:7)*, takes any seat of offense out of our hearts that the devil was intending to sit on.

Who made you do it? Nobody "made you do it" because if the desire wasn't in you, you wouldn't have done it! You can't make a non-drinker drink, you can't make a non-smoker smoke and you can't make a non-cusser cuss. You can't make anyone do anything that's not already in them! You can't make anyone act out a lust that is not already inside of them waiting to be acted out *(James 1:12-16)*.

Many people are sick mentally and physically because of unforgiveness. Just like the Holy Spirit comes to make habitation inside of us, the devil also wishes to do the same. "Christ is being formed in you" *(Galatians 4:19)*, meaning this is a process, not a one-time transaction. We cannot keep sinning and think that Jesus is being formed in us. So, in order to make ourselves devil-proof, we have to ask this question: What seats do we have available in our heart for the devil to sit on?

Forgiveness Must Be Finished

There is no such thing as being forgiven and still reserving your right to forgive other people for their wrongs against you. I have met so many brothers and sisters who think it is OK to be Christians who have been forgiven by God but have not yet forgiven the people in their lives who have done bad things to them. Whether it's with a mother, father, sister, brother or any other relationship in your life, unforgiveness is **not** an option.

There is no such thing as a knock-off salvation; you have to have the real thing. I understand that some pain is deeply rooted and some wounds go very deep in the heart, but ultimately the root of unforgiveness is PRIDE! Pride turns your lenses inside out and makes it all about **you** — what they did to **you** and how they hurt **you** and didn't accept **you** or let **you** in (and so forth). All of those things are doorkeepers to unforgiveness. When God brings true salvation, He brings true forgiveness.

You can only wear one outfit at a time. You are either taking one off to put on the other, or you're trying to make one fit over the other — but it never does. You can only serve one master at a time. So, if we see our thoughts as clothes, we cannot take salvation and wear it on top of unforgiveness. We have to repent first, take off unforgiveness and then put on salvation. You are either a son or a slave to sin with an Orphan Spirit.

The challenge is that when we don't deal with our inner issues, we hide them and try to cover them up and claim to be whole when we are not. Somehow, we think that it is OK to be Christians and still live in unforgiveness, bitterness, hate and all manner of disobedience. We are praying for breakthrough, but our heart is not true — so the first thing you have to break through is *you*!

I repeat: Unforgiveness is not an option!

> *Matthew 6:14 (AMP)* — *"For if you forgive others their trespasses [their reckless and willful sins], your heavenly Father will also forgive you. [15] But if you do not forgive others [nurturing your hurt and anger with the result that it interferes with your relationship with God], then your Father will not forgive your trespasses."*

Make things right first, then pray!

> *Mark 11:25 (AMP)* — *"Whenever you stand praying, if you have anything against anyone, forgive him [drop the issue, let it go], so that your Father who is in heaven will also forgive you your transgressions and wrongdoings [against Him and others]. [26] [But if you do not forgive, neither will your Father in heaven forgive your transgressions]."*

You are in danger of hellfire when you walk in unforgiveness!

Matthew 5:22 (AMP) — "But I say to you that everyone who continues to be angry with his brother or harbors malice against him shall be guilty before the court; and whoever speaks [contemptuously and insultingly] to his brother, 'Raca (You empty-headed idiot)!' shall be guilty before the supreme court (Sanhedrin); and whoever says, 'You fool!' shall be in danger of the fiery hell. ²³ So if you are presenting your offering at the altar, and while there you remember that your brother has something [such as a grievance or legitimate complaint] against you, ²⁴ leave your offering there at the altar and go. First make peace with your brother, and then come and present your offering."

Oftentimes we give God what we can spare in our flesh and what we're comfortable with. God wants what we're uncomfortable with giving. This is what being a living sacrifice is all about. God doesn't want what you have; He wants what has you. God appreciates your offering, but what He wants is your obedience.

1 Samuel 15:22 — "And Samuel said, Hath the LORD as great delight in burnt offerings and sacrifices, as in obeying the voice of the LORD? Behold, to obey is better than sacrifice, and to hearken than the fat of rams."

When you are rebellious, rebellion makes perfect sense to you because it is literally "the spirit that worketh in the children of disobedience." So then, when God says to do things one way and your mind says to do them another way, it makes perfect sense for you to ignore the voice of God.

"And You Shall Receive Power"

> *Acts 1:8 — "But ye shall receive power, after that the Holy Ghost is come upon you: and ye shall be witnesses unto me both in Jerusalem, and in all Judaea, and in Samaria, and unto the uttermost part of the earth."*

What is power? Power is God giving you the ability to:

1. Expect – Walk in an attitude and atmosphere of expectation.
2. Believe – The capacity to believe the promises of God and take Him at His word.
3. Do – To put action with your faith.

Power vs. Fear

Fear paralyzes us from taking action and takes away our ability to act on the Word of God.

> *2 Timothy 1:7 — "For God has not given us a spirit of fear, but of power, and of love and of a sound mind."*

The word "fear" in the Greek means "cowardice," signifying the lack of bravery and courage. "Courage is the state of showing mental or moral strength to persevere and withstand danger or difficulty"[9]. When there is a problem, God is not worried because He is the answer and solution. Nothing brings fear upon Him and neither did He give us that spirit, for it is a product of darkness.

God gave us power, which in the Greek is *dunamis*: "the inherent power, the power to reproduce itself, implying the need of constant activity and use for continued reproduction"[10]

. The power that dwells in us and that should be allowed (partnered with) is the Holy Spirit. This is the power that is in us to accomplish all things in the Kingdom. So, who do we constantly need to develop a relationship with to keep that power going? The Holy Spirit.

Ephesians 3:20 — "Now unto HIM that is able to do exceeding abundantly above all that we ask or think, according to the power that worketh IN us." (emphasis ours)

The power to overcome fear is not found in ourselves, but it's in the Holy Spirit and His ability to overcome anything. We just have to give Him permission in our lives to be able to fight on our behalf. The Holy Spirit will always point you to Jesus, who is "the way, the truth and the life." He gives us the power to put on Christ, to step into the mind of a Conqueror and be washed in His blood.

The Holy Spirit's power works in us, but He will not work in us *without us*. He is not there for you to control but for you to yield to His ways, that He may show you what offering and sacrifice should be made on your part. You can't submit to someone you're trying to control. A lot of times we want to submit *and* be God at the same time. Partnership requires relationship and submission.

Stir It Up

In *2 Timothy 1:6*, Paul tells his spiritual son Timothy, **"Wherefore I put thee in remembrance that thou stir up the gift of God, which is in thee by the putting on of my hands."** The Greek verb "stir up" is *anazopurein*, which means "to kindle up (the fire)." Paul, as a spiritual father, was someone with the authority and anointing to stir up the gifts of God in Timothy. God will always align your life with individuals who He will anoint specifically to stir up and bring out the gifts that He has given you.

In every season, God has brought the most unlikely of friendships and connections that I needed at that time, to sow seeds, give revelations about the gifts of God within me and teach me how to keep the fire lit. God showed me the analogy of a drink that has to be constantly stirred or else the good contents that make the drink flavorful and powerful will fall to the bottom. If not, when it gets poured out, you're only getting a watered-down substance. The drink must be stirred continuously and ready to be poured out with the quality, substance and purpose that it was put together to achieve.

How many of us are pouring out a watered-down substance because we have neglected the responsibility to stir? It's sad to see today that this is often what people are getting from the pulpit, the worship and the leaders who are supposed to keep their fire lit to empower God's people.

Our work doesn't stop once we receive the gifts, for it now has to be stewarded. The key to maintaining that "stirring" is relationship. Relationship with who? The Holy Spirit. The less we relate to Him, the lower the flame and the higher the potential of it going out will be. We have to get in His presence, fellowship with Him and yield to Him, and then we are able to partner with Him in learning those gifts and maintaining that fire.

The Oil of Joy for Mourning and Beauty for Ashes

We have to break up with the lie!

In order to exchange the oil of joy for mourning, you have to break up with the lie that you are currently in a relationship with. See yourself right now arm-and-arm with whatever lie that the devil has been using to keep you paralyzed and stuck in your old situation. It's like being in a bad relationship for way too long.

In the spirit realm, I see your soul like a record on a record player. On that record are recordings of your experiences, where you have a scratch or maybe multiple scratches that keep playing over and over again in your life. You're good for a while, everything's OK, and then all of a sudden, you have a mood change, a negative shift, depression, anxiety, stress — and you don't even know why. You just ran into one of your scratches, a place in your soul marked by an experience that is unresolved. These unresolved issues will play over and over again until they are healed.

What is your lie? Are you partnering with fear, doubt, unbelief, discouragement, oppression or depression? Do you have a contract with the enemy that says you're not enough, you're not worth it or you don't deserve happiness? It's time to break those contracts.

In the spirit I see the Lord standing in front of you right now, arm-and-arm with opportunity. You can see the opportunities now that have been around you all this time — because right now we break off of you every bad relationship, every satanic and demonic force that you have been partnering with, whether known or unknown, hidden or out in the open.

We now announce that you are divorced from those lies, in Jesus' name, and we declare over you a new covenant, a new contract with Jesus.

Jesus is bringing you in front of the Father at this very moment, and the Father is looking at you eye-to-eye, saying that you are a king, you are royalty, you are a brand plucked out of the fire to show forth His Glory. You are a king made in the image of the King of kings. This is your identity. This is your new ID card. This is your operating system in Jesus' name!

It's Not About You!

Once you realize that it's not about you and that your story is all about Jesus, you can cut off the desires of the flesh along with its claim to receive retribution. Your justice lies in your forgiveness and your understanding that you are being made an offering. We have the incredible opportunity to sow into the sacrifice that Jesus became for us. Jesus knew that He had to suffer, but He also knew that what was happening to Him wasn't about Him — it was about us. A seed had to be sown into the ground to die, so that many sons could achieve sonship through His sacrifice.

Everyone is going through something in life, and it's so easy to fall into the "woe is me" syndrome, throw a pity party or keep telling your story to everyone who is willing to hear it. You keep getting energy from your story, but it's not healing energy... It's a demonic energy that actually gives energy and worship to the enemy as you keep recounting what happened to you without declaring the death, burial and resurrection of the situation. If you can't say, "It was good for me that I have been afflicted," then you have not yet been healed from your past. Cut off the ego, cut off the rights of the flesh — and take on "the fellowship of His suffering" — that you may know the power of His resurrection.

> *Isaiah 53:7 — "He was oppressed, and he was afflicted, yet he opened not his mouth: he is brought as a lamb to the slaughter, and as a sheep before her shearers is dumb, so he openeth not his mouth. [8] He was taken from prison and from judgment: and who shall declare his*

generation? for he was cut off out of the land of the living: for the transgression of my people was he stricken. ⁹ And he made his grave with the wicked, and with the rich in his death; because he had done no violence, neither was any deceit in his mouth. ¹⁰ Yet it pleased the LORD to bruise him; he hath put him to grief: when thou shalt make his soul an offering for sin, he shall see his seed, he shall prolong his days, and the pleasure of the LORD shall prosper in his hand. ¹¹ He shall see of the travail of his soul, and shall be satisfied: by his knowledge shall my righteous servant justify many; for he shall bear their iniquities. ¹² Therefore will I divide him a portion with the great, and he shall divide the spoil with the strong; because he hath poured out his soul unto death: and he was numbered with the transgressors; and he bare the sin of many, and made intercession for the transgressors."

Never discount what you have been through. The act of crushing is used to produce oil. The crushing is not comfortable; it is unexpected and oftentimes lasts longer than you want it to. God is in charge of your winepress, and He is the lover of your soul. He knows how much you can take, He knows your destination and He knows how to stretch you in order to make you what you need to be to reach that destination.

When we look at our pain and understand its purpose, a transaction is made. It is the exchange where we see the oil of joy. Now in this crushing, I can see the oil. I can smell the perfume of Mary Magdalene. Here I see a kind of worship that can only come out of ashes. This is a worship that comes when the incense is burning. Your life is that incense.

There are no mistakes in your life — the Author and Finisher of your faith has calculated every twist, every turn, every mountain, every valley, every pitfall and every promotion that you are going to experience in your life. Nothing in your life is by happenstance; God has strategically planned every step of your walk. Your mistakes, your disobedience and your obedience have already been factored in. And you know this because He has worked all things together for your good *(Romans 8:28)*.

The oil of joy is contagious, outrageous and advantageous. The oil of joy is just like it sounds: It's thick, sticky and gets on everything. When I think of it, the oil is like thick syrup being poured onto pancakes. It is sweet, it soaks into the pancake and it has become one with the pancake. Do you now understand what it means when the Bible describes Jesus Christ? Jesus is the pancake and Christ is the syrup. When we are covered in His anointing, we are covered with the pancake syrup of Heaven.

David said, "O taste and see that the Lord is good" *(Psalm 34:8)*. When God gave Israel manna from Heaven, it tasted like honey in their mouths. Whenever we give people something that comes from Heaven, it should have God's sweetness on it. If you are an ambassador of the Kingdom of Heaven, you should have God's sweetness on you.

The true Word and love of God is not religious, bringing people again into bondage. The love of God, our Father, is the most beautiful thing you can imagine. It is the family reunion of all family reunions. It is the restoration of slaves into their kingship. It is the realized destiny and purpose of the sons of God. Heaven every day! *Oh, the joy that comes from being restored to the Father!* Everything that the Father, the Son and the Holy Spirit have done is in order to get us back into relationship with Them. Being connected with the Father is Heaven on earth, joy that is unspeakable and full of glory, being immersed in the actual Kingdom and culture of Heaven.

The Garment of Praise

Put on thy strength, O Israel. Put on the garment of praise.

> *Isaiah 61:1 — "The Spirit of the Lord GOD is upon me; because the LORD hath anointed me to preach good tidings unto the meek; he hath sent me to bind up the brokenhearted, to proclaim liberty to the captives, and the opening of the prison to them that are bound; ² To proclaim the acceptable year of the LORD, and the day of vengeance of our God; to comfort all that mourn; ³ To appoint unto them that mourn in Zion, to give unto them beauty for ashes, the oil of joy for mourning, the garment of praise for the spirit of heaviness; that they might be called trees of righteousness, the planting of the LORD, that he might be glorified."*

Let's be honest: You don't feel like praising all the time. Sometimes heaviness just walks right up to you, pulls up a chair and pours itself a glass of tea. And before you know it, you two are talking about old times. And somewhere during the tea party, you take a look around, and depression and discouragement have joined the conversation. And then somebody puts their arm around your neck, and slothfulness kindly escorts you to the bed. Before you know it, you have been sleeping for hours and hours. Hours turn into days, days turn into weeks and weeks turn into months.

This is the strategy that the enemy uses to steal, kill and destroy our lives. The antidote to that is PRAISE! King

David was such a model for going through bad times with the right attitude.

> *1 Samuel 30:1 — "And it came to pass, when David and his men were come to Ziklag on the third day, that the Amalekites had invaded the south, and Ziklag, and smitten Ziklag, and burned it with fire; ²And had taken the women captives, that were therein: they slew not any, either great or small, but carried them away, and went on their way. ³So David and his men came to the city, and, behold, it was burned with fire; and their wives, and their sons, and their daughters, were taken captives. ⁴Then David and the people that were with him lifted up their voice and wept, until they had no more power to weep. ⁵And David's two wives were taken captives, Ahinoam the Jezreelitess, and Abigail the wife of Nabal the Carmelite. ⁶And David was greatly distressed; for the people spake of stoning him, because the soul of all the people was grieved, every man for his sons and for his daughters: but David encouraged himself in the LORD his God."*

Your circumstances and situations will be there until you change your response. Praise is a garment that must be intentionally put on. Praise is not an emotion; it is a decision. Based on how well you know God, you will look at the circumstances that have presented themselves to you, and you have a decision to make. Is God a good Father or not? Has God brought you out of trials before or not? This is where you remember the bear and the lion as you face your giant *(1 Samuel 17:34-37)*. Fear makes you forget; faith makes you remember. Faith is the ability to remember what God has already done for you.

Praise is the tenacious decision to glorify God no matter what situation you're in. When you choose to praise, you are no longer moved by your external experience, for you are being moved by your internal knowing of the Father. His goodness is your compass, and after a while you no longer doubt it. A son knows his father, like Isaac knew Abraham and Jesus knew His heavenly Father. A son learns how to remove all fear, doubt and unbelief through a perfect love that is developed over time. A son is obedient even when it's not convenient. A son is adamant about pleasing the Father, and praise is the offering of sonship. Praise was not an option for King David. It was an expression of his continual trust and love for God. No wonder God said that David was a man after His own heart *(1 Samuel 13:14)*.

Jesus, The Perfect Son

This morning I woke up to the Holy Spirit hovering over me, and I knew immediately that He wanted to give me something. I lifted my hands to soak in His presence and listened. No words from myself, unless He instructed me to declare something, but 99 percent just listening.

As I listened, I heard the Holy Spirit say, "You can't have the Kingdom unless you have God the Father." This made perfect sense to me, because how can you have the Kingdom if you don't have the King? Jesus said, "No man cometh unto the Father but by the Son." So, the destination is not the Son; it's the Father. But you can't get to the Father just by going to the Son. You must become like the Son. Jesus is the key, and His example is what we are meant to imitate. His way is our way to the Father.

The devil has been using religion to steal, kill and destroy people's lives by not telling us the truth. We are taught that everything is Jesus focused and about us getting saved from our sins, so that we can go to Heaven — and that is not the whole truth. This is not the fullness of what Jesus came to preach, and it is not the only reason why God deposited His greatest gift, the Holy Spirit, inside of us. Jesus came to earth as the perfect Son of God to pay for our sins, taking onto Himself all the judgments that came upon our lives because of sin, so that we could be free and He could show us Father God, our Creator, as the "Good Father" that He really is.

Every story in the Bible, everything that Jesus did and everything that we do as Christians is supposed to show and reconnect this world to God the Father. This is the Kingdom of God! Bringing God, the Father's sons back into love, communion and inheritance with Him. Showing the world that they are not orphans who have been abandoned into a world of brokenness, poverty, debt, lack, want, sickness, infirmity, disease, murder and death. We are sons of the Most High God, our Father who has adopted us and given us the Spirit of Adoption, the Holy Spirit, "whereby we cry, 'Abba Father'" *(Romans 8:15)*.

The three things that Jesus died to do:

1. Atone for our sins.
2. Take our judgments onto Himself.
3. Return us into relationship and communion with God the Father.

Romans 8:1 — "There is therefore now no condemnation to them which are in Christ Jesus, who walk not after the flesh, but after the Spirit. [2] For the law of the Spirit of life in Christ Jesus hath made me free from the law of sin and death."

The Spirit of Adoption

The Spirit of Adoption is a fruit of the Holy Spirit. The fruits of the Holy Spirit are something that are produced, whereas gifts of the Holy Spirit are given to you. Both fruits and gifts must be developed and unfolded overtime in relationship with the Holy Spirit. Receiving the Spirit of Adoption is a fruit that is developed after receiving the Holy Spirit and is cultivated through relationship as we walk with God. This is why proper discipleship is necessary in order for any Christian to develop into maturity, according to *Ephesians 4:12*. There are Fruit and Gifts of the Holy Spirit that become available to us after we receive the Baptism of the Holy Spirit. These fruit and gifts are not automatic, they must be studied out, and pursued, according to, *1 Corinthians 14:1;*

> *"Follow after charity, and desire spiritual gifts."*

> Romans *8:14-15* — *"For as many as are led by the Spirit of God, they are the sons of God. [15]For ye have not received the spirit of bondage again to fear; but ye have received the Spirit of adoption, whereby we cry, Abba, Father."*

The prayer of Salvation does not automatically turn us into sons of God, it qualifies us to become one if we are willing to be led by the Holy Spirit until our sonship is developed. Many are called to sonship, but few are chosen. *(Romans 8:21-25; Matthew 22:14)*

Having the Spirit of Adoption is just like being filled with the Holy Spirit. If you don't have it, you don't have it. One of the evidences of being filled with the Holy Spirit is speaking in tongues, and the evidence of having the Spirit of Adoption is being able to truly cry out, "Abba Father," "Daddy God." And just like being filled with the Holy Spirit, you know when you are filled with the Spirit of Adoption because you have received a revelation that God truly is your Father and Daddy.

As much as you want to, as good as your intentions may be, you cannot cry out, "Abba Father," until you have the Spirit of Adoption by the Holy Spirit. The affection in your heart is reconnected to God the Father, and the union that was broken through Adam and Eve's sin has now been restored through salvation in Jesus Christ.

People assume when they get saved that they automatically have the Spirit of Adoption, but that is not correct. If it were true, then creation would not be groaning as it is waiting for the manifestation (maturation) of the sons of God. Being a son of God is a revelation that only the Holy Spirit can give to you. How do you get this revelation? By walking out your salvation until the Holy Spirit sees the heart of a son, like He did with Abraham and Isaac on the altar.

Similarly, even though Jacob had received the birthright, he was called to be a son and chosen by God. He could not become Israel until he was processed in the wilderness. After he passed the process, the Angel told him, "NOW you are a prince with men and with God," and Jacob's name was changed to Israel, the Chosen One. Many are called, but few are chosen. Chosen sons stand on the other side of the process. Don't give up while you're in the process. Wrestle with God until you see your change come *(Genesis 32:24-30)*.

The Powerful Transformation of the Holy Spirit

The only One who can give you Kingdom glasses is the Holy Spirit. We have been taught that the Holy Spirit is the down payment of a greater gift that we get from God.

> *Ephesians 1:14 (CEB) — "The Holy Spirit is the down payment on our inheritance, which is applied toward our redemption as God's own people, resulting in the honor of God's glory."*

The Kingdom of God is inside the Holy Spirit, and the Holy Spirit is inside of us. The Holy Spirit is the One who introduces and teaches us the principles of the Kingdom of God.

> *Acts 1:6 — "When they therefore were come together, they asked of him, saying, Lord, wilt thou at this time restore again the kingdom to Israel? ⁷ And he said unto them, It is not for you to know the times or the seasons, which the Father hath put in his own power. ⁸ But ye shall receive power, after that the Holy Ghost is come upon you: and ye shall be witnesses unto me both in Jerusalem, and in all Judaea, and in Samaria, and unto the uttermost part of the earth."*

> *Luke 17:20 — "And when he was demanded of the Pharisees, when the kingdom of God should come, he answered them and said, The kingdom of God cometh not with observation. ²¹ Neither shall they say, Lo here! or, lo there! for, behold, the kingdom of God is within you."*

Religious people are looking for a building or a location for God to restore His Kingdom in, but God is looking for a people to put His Kingdom inside.

The disciples asked Jesus if He would presently restore the Kingdom to Israel. Jesus responded, "You will receive power after the Holy Spirit has come upon you." This power that Jesus spoke of was the power of the Kingdom of Heaven, the Holy Spirit. For three and a half years Jesus had given the disciples the Word of God, and He told them, *"I will pray the Father and He shall give you another Comforter, that He may abide with you forever" (John 14:16)*. The other Comforter was the Holy Spirit, who would then answer the question that the disciples asked Jesus in *Acts 1* by teaching them the Kingdom of Heaven. The Holy Spirit is the Kingdom of Heaven that we are filled with when we are baptized in the Spirit *(Luke 17:20-21)*.

During His ministry Jesus was depositing parts into the shopping carts of the disciples. The funny thing is that the disciples did not understand what Jesus was saying most of the time, but Jesus did not let that deter Him from preparing those 12 disciples to be containers of His Kingdom. So, even as *1 Corinthians 13* mentions, everything we learn is "in part" until "that which is perfect comes" and "that which is in part is done away."

Transformation comes from the revelations that are given to us as the Holy Spirit turns the water of the Word into His wine. Jesus' first miracle was at the wedding feast in Cana *(John 2:1-11)*, which is symbolic of the wedding feast for the Bride of Christ *(Luke 14:15-23)*. Water is symbolic of the Word *(Ephesians 5:26)*, and wine is symbolic of revelation *(1 Corinthians 11:26; Mark 14:22-27)*.

The Word of God is hidden in the *Logos*, until it is revealed in the *Rhema* by the Holy Spirit. The revealing of the Word of God by the Holy Spirit is wine — the *Rhema* Word of God. This means that the perfect love of the Father is administered through the guidance of the Holy Spirit. Without the Holy Spirit, all we can get from any man is religious parts. Even a church sermon is only the water of the Word until the Holy Spirit changes it from water into wine. So, you can go to church as much as you want, because one man is planting and one man is watering, but only God can give the increase to what we are doing.

> *Zechariah 4:6 — "Then he answered and spake unto me, saying, This is the word of the LORD unto Zerubbabel, saying, Not by might, nor by power, but by my spirit, saith the LORD of hosts."*

God makes everything beautiful in **its** time. Everything has a time and a season, a rhyme and a reason. But God is the one who blesses whatever efforts that we put into developing our relationship with Him. There is no way to fool God; there is no way around Him, above Him or below Him!

That **BEAUTIFUL** Holy Spirit of God, He is the One who decides when we are ready. He is the One who gives us revelation to a chapter that we have read over and over again, and all of a sudden it leaps off the pages and we now understand it. He is the One who enlightens the eyes of our understanding and helps us to realize the hope of our calling in Him. Information is just knowledge without the Holy Spirit, but with Him it becomes revelation. Information is just religion without revelation.

The Holy Spirit is the One who reveals the Bible to us. The Bible is a book of relationship that cannot be understood without God's Spirit. So, if you're reading your Bible and you can't understand it, it's time to partner with the Holy Spirit. Ask God to fill you with His Holy Spirit, and in quietness learn the sound of His voice. Humble yourself like a little child, put your hand in His hand and get ready to discover the Kingdom of Heaven. The Holy Spirit is our Tour Guide, our Compass, our GPS (God Positioning System).

The Pathway into the Kingdom

When you lose the kid, you lose the Kingdom.
When you lose the King, you lose the Kingdom.

When you lose the kid in you, you lose the way into the Kingdom, because Jesus said, "Unless you become like this little child, you will in no wise enter my kingdom." When you lose the King, you lose the Kingdom, because the Kingdom is the culture and habitation of the King. We often hear about "Kingdom culture," but we must realize that this very Kingdom culture is what God the Father built for Adam and Eve in the Garden of Eden. They lost the Kingdom because they lost the kid (childlike obedience and expectation), which was the key to enter into the Kingdom.

So, right now, if we're not in the Kingdom, we must follow Jesus' example of being the Kid, the Son with childlike expectation, only doing those things that He saw the Father doing. This is how you can be living on earth and living life in the Kingdom at the same time.

The Pathway Out of the Kingdom

How did satan lose the Kingdom of God?

➤ He stopped being a kid (being led by the Father).
➤ He stopped following God (lost his purpose).
➤ He stopped being obedient (entered into the Spirit of Rebellion, which is witchcraft).
➤ He opened his heart to pride (then he fell).
➤ He started having ambitions outside of God's purpose for him (lost his identity).
➤ He lost the fear of the Lord (lost his reverence for God).
➤ He started doubting God (second-guessing).
➤ He started walking in deception (darkness became his habitation).
➤ He took God's things and started using them for his own purpose in glory (became a thief).
➤ He manipulated God's creations for his own glory (creator of abominations).

Isaiah 14:12-17 — "How art thou fallen from heaven, O Lucifer, son of the morning! how art thou cut down to the ground, which didst weaken the nations! [13] For thou hast said in thine heart, I will ascend into heaven, I will exalt my throne above the stars of God: I will sit also upon the mount of the congregation, in the sides of the north: [14] I will ascend above the heights of the clouds; I will be like the most High. [15] Yet thou shalt be brought down to hell, to the sides of the pit. [16] They that see thee shall narrowly look upon thee, and consider thee, saying, Is this the man that made the earth to tremble, that did shake kingdoms; [17] That made the world as a wilderness, and destroyed the cities thereof; that opened not the house of his prisoners?"

Key Points

1. Jesus is the R.E. (redeemer, restorer, resurrection, reconciliation, etc.), and the devil is the D.E. (deceiver, destructor, delusion, etc.). *(John 10:10)*
2. Forgiveness is not optional. *(Matthew 6:14-15)*
3. Power is the ability to expect, to believe and to do. *(Acts 1:8; 2 Timothy 1:7)*
4. You must break up with the lie that you're believing and recognize that it's not all about you. *(Isaiah 53:7-12)*
5. Praise is a garment that must be intentionally put on. Praise is not an emotion; it is a decision. *(Isaiah 61; 1 Samuel 30)*
6. Jesus is the perfect Son and the example that we are to follow to sonship. *(John 8:28-29)*
7. Every story in the Bible, everything that Jesus did and everything that we do as Christians are supposed to show and reconnect this world to God the Father. This is the Kingdom of God! *(Romans 8)*
8. You cannot cry out, "Abba, Father," until you have the Spirit of Adoption by the Holy Spirit. *(Romans 8:15)*
9. The Word of God is hidden in the *Logos*, until it is revealed in the *Rhema* by the Holy Spirit. *(John 1:14, 6:63)*

Notes

Notes

_____

_____

_____

_____

_____

_____

_____

_____

_____

_____

_____

_____

_____

_____

_____

_____

_____

_____

_____

_____

_____

Notes

_____
_____
_____
_____
_____
_____
_____
_____
_____
_____
_____
_____
_____
_____
_____
_____
_____
_____
_____
_____
_____
_____

CHAPTER 7: THE SON

From the Pigpen to the Palace

When we look at the story of "The Prodigal Son," we have often heard it preached as a story of a sinner coming back to God. The truth of the matter is that the story of the Prodigal Son is the story of mankind making its way back to the Father. In Adam we ALL fell and we ALL walked away from the Father in him. We were ALL born in sin, shaped in iniquity, out of covenant with God, orphans and FATHERLESS!

> *Luke 15:20 (AMP) — "So he got up and came to his father. But while he was still a long way off, his father saw him and was moved with compassion for him, and ran and embraced him and kissed him. [21] And the son said to him, 'Father, I have sinned against heaven and in your sight; I am no longer worthy to be called your son.' [22] But the father said to his servants, 'Quickly*

> bring out the best robe [for the guest of honor] and put
> it on him; and give him a ring for his hand, and sandals
> for his feet. [23] And bring the fattened calf and slaughter
> it, and let us [invite everyone and] feast and
> celebrate."

Adam put mankind into the pigpen when he partnered with satan and rebelled against God. Like the wayward son, we were hired as servants and brought so low that we were ready to eat what the pigs eat. All of mankind had divorced themselves from God their Father and Creator. We were living outside of our purpose, outside of our identity and outside of our destiny.

And then a hand reaches in — it is the hand of Jesus, the Son of God, the Lamb that was crucified before the foundation of the world. Knowing that humans could not redeem themselves, God sent His only begotten Son who would take Adam's place in the pigpen and begin our journey back to the Father.

> *2 Corinthians 5:21 (ESV)* — *"For our sake he made him to be sin who knew no sin, so that in him we might become the righteousness of God."*

We all came into this world with a fake ID (because of Adam and Eve's fall). The detriment of this fake ID is our missed calling, lost identity and living a life outside of purpose. We couldn't come to the Father by ourselves, so Jesus, the perfect Son who was already one with the Father, brought us back to Him. Now we have the opportunity to use Jesus' name and His ID.

> *2 Corinthians 8:9* — *"For ye know the grace of our Lord Jesus Christ, that, though he was rich, yet for your sakes he became poor, that ye through his poverty might be rich."*

John 12:24 — "Verily, verily, I say unto you, Except a corn of wheat fall into the ground and die, it abideth alone: but if it die, it bringeth forth much fruit. He that loveth his life shall lose it; and he that hateth his life in this world shall keep it unto life eternal."

Like a grain of wheat, Jesus died and was planted so that we could become His fruit.

Romans 6:3 — "Know ye not, that so many of us as were baptized into Jesus Christ were baptized into his death? ⁴ Therefore we are buried with him by baptism into death: that like as Christ was raised up from the dead by the glory of the Father, even so we also should walk in newness of life."

The Children of the devil

In *John 8:42-47*, Jesus engaged in an interesting conversation with the religious leaders who were seeking to kill Him. These were children of Israel, the Chosen Ones, considered to be the Church at that time. They said, "Abraham is our father," but Jesus responded, "You are of your father the devil".

Things that Jesus told the religious leaders:
1. If God were your father, you would love me.
2. You don't understand my speech.
3. You cannot hear my words.
4. The devil is your father.
5. There is no truth in the devil.
6. You will do the lusts of your father.
7. The devil is a murderer.
8. The devil is the father of liars.
9. The truth is not in you.

135

10. You will not abide in the truth.
11. You cannot be a believer.
12. You are not of God.

Who's Your Daddy?
(Revelations That God Spoke Into Us)

➤ You can choose to receive the Spirit of Adoption, which allows you to cry out, "Abba Father," or you can choose to receive the Spirit of Rebellion, aligned with satan as your father.

➤ God was essentially saying to Adam in the Garden of Eden, "The day that you choose to sin against me, you will switch fathers!"

➤ In the instance of Cain and Abel, each of their offerings showed who their father was.

➤ Cain failed the same test that his dad had failed. The generational curse had already started.

The Path of Salvation:

Jesus is the truth, and as the Bride of Christ we choose to be married to the truth. If we desire to know and abide in the truth, God is our Father.

The Path of Damnation:

The devil is a liar and the father of lies! We can also choose to be married to a lie if we refuse the truth. The killer of truth is someone who chooses to be married to a lie. If we desire to accept and abide in lies, the devil becomes our father.

The Birth of Religion

The moral of the story is that it's not enough to go where God already went — we have to be where He **is**. The devil's strategy is to build a camp where God used to be and to hire religious people to build religions. A religion can be any denomination that purposely chooses to follow the doctrines of man instead of the Holy Spirit. When we follow men and not the Holy Spirit, we open ourselves up to be possessed by other spirits that are demonic and religious in nature. These religious spirits are familiar with the ways of church and carry on just like a church service. What these services lack is the transformative renewing, refreshing and life-giving power of the Holy Spirit. These services are counterfeits of a Spirit-led service and are consequently full of lust, perversion, deception, lies, envy, strife and division.

> *2 Timothy 3:1 (NIV)* — *"But mark this: There will be terrible times in the last days. ² People will be lovers of themselves, lovers of money, boastful, proud, abusive, disobedient to their parents, ungrateful, unholy, ³ without love, unforgiving, slanderous, without self-control, brutal, not lovers of the good, ⁴ treacherous, rash, conceited, lovers of pleasure rather than lovers of God— ⁵ having a form of godliness but denying its power. Have nothing to do with such people. They are the kind who worm their way into homes and gain control over gullible women, who are loaded down with sins and are swayed by all kinds of evil desires, ⁷ always learning but never able to come to a knowledge of the truth. ⁸ Just as Jannes and Jambres opposed Moses, so also these teachers oppose the truth. They are men of depraved minds, who, as far as the faith is concerned,*

are rejected. [9] But they will not get very far because, as in the case of those men, their folly will be clear to everyone."

The Children of God

The Old Testament proved that we could not get to God on our own just by following the Law. The children of Israel failed over and over again. Jesus came to accomplish what Adam and Eve failed to do. When we receive salvation and allow ourselves through the Holy Spirit to put on Christ, we enter and live through His victory.

2 Corinthians 5:17 — "Therefore if any man be in Christ, he is a new creature: old things are passed away; behold, all things are become new."

Now, despite Jesus having paid for salvation, unfortunately creation is still groaning and waiting for the sons of God to realize who they are. When we receive salvation, we say a prayer that acknowledges who God is and what Jesus died to pay for. This qualifies us to begin the class or process of becoming sons of God. The prayer of salvation is not the arrival; it is only the beginning of the journey.

The Vision of Salvation

I see the moment of salvation in a vision: We just prayed and accepted God's invitation to be washed in the blood of His Son, Jesus Christ — and *pow!* — a gun goes off. We have now passed from death into life; we are new creations in Christ Jesus and have come out of darkness into His marvelous light. We have been born again, but the thing to remember is that the term "born again" means exactly what it sounds like. We are now spiritual babies who must grow and mature into sonship. The process of growth happens over time.

So, when we heard the gun go off, it wasn't time to sit down — it was time to start running! The Bible says, "The race is not to the swift, nor the battle to the strong," but rather to those who endure to the end *(Ecclesiastes 9:11; Hebrews 12:1)*. The journey has just begun when we pray for salvation, and we get to choose if we are going to be in the Outer Court, the Inner Court or the Holy of Holies. We get to choose how much time and availability that we are going to give to God every day to make us into vessels that He can use.

Becoming a son of God is not an entitlement that we get through praying for salvation; it is a privilege that must be desired and pursued. Many are called to be sons, but few are chosen. The huge problem with church is when people allow new believers to think that they are already at their destination when they prayed for salvation — not realizing that they are just at the beginning of their race. And that is when we conform to what we see around us in church, instead of being transformed through the maturation process of taking on a renewed mind.

It would be convenient if as soon as we prayed for salvation, we could consider ourselves sons of God. And I know what you're thinking: "I am already a son of God." But the truth and the reality of the matter is that we must follow Jesus into the Kingdom like that little child who He brought before the crowd in *Matthew 18:3*.

So, when Jesus showed them a little child, He was also showing them a doorway. On one side of the doorway is the Church, and on the other side of the doorway is the

Kingdom of God. Now, you must be in the Church in order to find the doorway into the Kingdom, and this is where the prayer of salvation comes in: to bring you into the Body of Christ. But the dangerous assumption is that because you're in the Church, you're doing Kingdom work.

Walking into the doorway of the Kingdom is a choice that Jesus presented to them. We must be intentional in order to become sons and in order to carry out the Kingdom. Jesus is called "the Way" because He is our example.

Jesus' Way to Sonship

1. Salvation

> *Romans 10:9 — "That if thou shalt confess with thy mouth the Lord Jesus, and shalt believe in thine heart that God hath raised him from the dead, thou shalt be saved. [10] For with the heart man believeth unto righteousness; and with the mouth confession is made unto salvation."*

2. Spirit-led Living

> *Romans 8:14 "For as many as are led by the Spirit of God, they are the sons of God."*

3. Discipleship

> *John 8:31 — "Then said Jesus to those Jews which believed on him, If ye continue in my word, then are ye my disciples indeed."*

4. Sonship

> *Romans 8:15 — "For ye have not received the spirit of bondage again to fear; but ye have received the Spirit of adoption, whereby we cry, Abba, Father."*

5. Kingdom

> *Matthew 6:33 — "But seek ye first the kingdom of God, and his righteousness; and all these things shall be added unto you."*

We are now following the example of Jesus, the Son of God, who became a curse for us and bore our sins on the cross. Jesus took that cross and turned it into a bridge, allowing us to make it back to the Father. Now that the prodigal sons of the earth have returned to the Father, we are now eligible for our full inheritance in God. Creation is groaning, waiting for us to walk in the fullness of what God has for us. Now it's time to get back to the Garden of Eden, fellowship with our Father and have the Glory of God restored to our lives. The Bible says that in the end days the earth will be full of the Glory of the Lord.

> *Habakkuk 2:14 — "For the earth shall be filled with the knowledge of the glory of the LORD, as the waters cover the sea."*

The Anointing

Have you ever felt like you were the right person in the wrong place? Have you ever felt that if you could just get the right opportunity that matched your gifts, skills and education, you could flourish? Well, of course you could! Imagine if your arm was where your leg is or if your ear was where your nose is. You would be faced with the challenge of having the right part in the wrong place.

We were all born and called to be the answer to certain questions that the world is asking. You are the answer to a specific question or set of questions, and no one can answer that question the way you can. This is why we should never make room for jealousy or comparison.

There are over 7.6 billion people on the earth, and no two people are alike. No two people have the same fingerprint, voice frequency or even the same eye biometrics. We are all given specific talents, gifts and motivations. We all have our own journey that creates a filter through which we see the world, and that makes each one of us unique. You can teach 100 people a song, but no one will sing the song the way you do. No one will paint a picture the way you imagine it, and no one will express a dance the way you can dance it. This is the beauty and gift of individuality that God has given to humanity. This is also called the anointing.

The spiritual definition of anointing means to pour on, rub into or to smear something on someone. When God anoints you, He literally puts Himself on you to enable you to do what you were born to do, like no one else can do it. When we refer to Jesus, we call Him Jesus *Christ*, which literally means "the Anointed One and His anointing." The Bible says that He is the "Christ in you, the hope of Glory":

> *Colossians 1:23 — "If ye continue in the faith grounded and settled, and be not moved away from the hope of the gospel, which ye have heard, and which was preached to every creature which is under heaven; whereof I Paul am made a minister...* [25] *according to the dispensation of God which is given to me for you, to fulfil the word of God;* [26] *Even the mystery which hath*

> been hid from ages and from generations, but now is made manifest to his saints: [27] To whom God would make known what is the riches of the glory of this mystery among the Gentiles; which is Christ in you, the hope of glory."

Christ was not Jesus' last name; it was the announcement of His anointing. When Jesus came on the scene, one of the first things that He did was announce what He was anointed to do. Up until this time, everything about Jesus was a prophecy, a promise, a hope not yet fulfilled. Jesus was and is the walking fulfillment of the promises of God to mankind, the reverse of every curse, the undoing of all the devil's works and the revelation of the goodness of the Father!

> Luke 4:18 — "The Spirit of the Lord is upon me, because he hath anointed me to preach the gospel to the poor; he hath sent me to heal the brokenhearted, to preach deliverance to the captives, and recovering of sight to the blind, to set at liberty them that are bruised, [19] To preach the acceptable year of the Lord."

Illumination

The announcement of that anointing was Jesus basically saying, "God has put Himself on me to accomplish these things." When we as human beings spend regular time with God as Jesus did daily on the mountaintop of relationship, we allow God to put Himself on us. When we lift our hands and surrender to the presence of God, we enter into His rest. When the Bible mentions the rest of God, it is referring to a place that we enter because of time spent regularly in His presence. This is not time spent talking; it is time spent resting, silently waiting on the presence of God to cover us.

This explains why Jesus was truly anointed — Jesus *Christ*. The *Christ* is God being poured on, rubbed into and smeared all over you. This is what a good shepherd does to his sheep: The anointing debugs, equips and recharges you. So, when God rubs Himself on you, He is rubbing His presence on you in such a way that demons have to flee from your life. This is called debugging. Also, His presence is where you receive your equipment, your spiritual armor. In His presence, with your hands lifted, is where your spiritual plug is plugged into the socket. This posture of lifting your hands up before God is very important.

1 Timothy 2:8 — "I will therefore that men pray everywhere, lifting up holy hands, without wrath and doubting."

This is not just a recommendation; it is a revelation of how sons get charged up and receive Son-light from the Father. Sons receive Son-light, recharging, equipping and debugging by waiting on the Lord in His presence. Some people call this "soaking," "tarrying" or "waiting on (and in) the presence of God." A transaction is happening while we wait in the presence of God with our hands uplifted.

Isaiah 40:31 — "But they that wait upon the LORD shall renew their strength; they shall mount up with wings as eagles; they shall run, and not be weary; and they shall walk, and not faint."

Exodus 17:11 — "And it came to pass, when Moses held up his hand, that Israel prevailed: and when he let down his hand, Amalek prevailed. 12 But Moses hands were heavy; and they took a stone, and put it under him, and he sat thereon; and Aaron and Hur stayed up his hands, the one on the one side, and the other on the other side; and his hands were steady until the going down of the sun."

Regular time spent with God in His presence is how we keep our anointing charged up and stay full of the Holy Spirit. Getting filled with the Holy Spirit is a continual relationship and communion that we have with God. It is not a one-time filling that stays full forever, just like one wedding ceremony does not keep you married for the duration of your marriage. It is a relationship that must be maintained on a regular basis with God.

This is the reason why many Christians don't have the relationship with God that they should have. We make an agreement with God at the beginning that we don't maintain through continual relationship. The Bible calls us "the Bride of Christ" with the revelation in mind that God wants to share with us a close and intimate relationship that must be intentionally maintained for success.

Ephesians 6:10 — "Finally, my brethren, be strong in the Lord, and in the power of his might. [11] Put on the whole armour of God, that ye may be able to stand against the wiles of the devil. [12] For we wrestle not against flesh and blood, but against principalities, against powers, against the rulers of the darkness of this world, against spiritual wickedness in high places. [13] Wherefore take unto you the whole armour of God, that ye may be able to withstand in the evil day, and having done all, to stand. [14] Stand therefore, having your loins girt about with truth, and having on the breastplate of righteousness; [15] And your feet shod with the preparation of the gospel of peace; [16] Above all, taking the shield of faith, wherewith ye shall be able to quench all the fiery darts of the wicked. [17] And take the helmet of salvation, and the sword of the Spirit, which *is the word of God: ¹⁸ Praying always with all prayer and supplication in the Spirit, and watching thereunto with all perseverance and supplication for all saints."*

Since we are talking about the anointing, Holy Spirit thought it was important for us to mention how to put on the full armor of God. We've heard this preached numerous times in church, but who tells you how to put it on? God is Spirit, so His armor is spiritual, and therefore the only way to put on His armor is to get it from the spirit realm. Waiting in the presence of the Lord causes God to coat you with His armor, to put His strength and His might on you *(Isaiah 40:31)*.

Each individual piece of spiritual armor has a different function, but it cannot be equipped by any physical means. You can't actually go to the store to buy the Helmet of Salvation or the Breastplate of Righteousness. God puts the armor on you as you wait in His presence. At the same time, the Holy Spirit is renewing your strength, and you are mounting up on spiritual wings as eagles (which means elevation). You are running but not becoming weary; you are walking long distances with God but not fainting. The anointing is the Holy Spirit's power smeared on you. The Holy Spirit is a quickening agent, force and power.

John 6:63 — "It is the spirit that quickeneth; the flesh profiteth nothing: the words that I speak unto you, they are spirit, and they are life."

The difference between life and death is the Holy Spirit!

Gifting vs. Anointing

There is a difference between being gifted and being anointed. In this book we are not going to go super in-depth about the gifts of the Spirit. This topic will be unfolded more in-depth in one of our future books, but what we will leave you with now is what Paul described to the Corinthians about spiritual gifts:

> *1 Corinthians 12:1 — "Now concerning spiritual gifts, brethren, I would not have you ignorant. ² Ye know that ye were Gentiles, carried away unto these dumb idols, even as ye were led. ³ Wherefore I give you to understand, that no man speaking by the Spirit of God calleth Jesus accursed: and that no man can say that Jesus is the Lord, but by the Holy Ghost. ⁴ Now there are diversities of gifts, but the same Spirit."*

3 Gifts of Power
- ➤ Faith
- ➤ Miracles
- ➤ Healing

3 Gifts of Revelation
- ➤ Words of Wisdom
- ➤ Words of Knowledge
- ➤ Discerning of Spirits

3 Gifts of Inspiration
- ➤ Prophecy
- ➤ Tongues
- ➤ Interpretation of Tongues

> *Romans 11:29 — "For the gifts and calling of God are without repentance."*

The anointing is for appointment. When God appoints you to do something, He anoints you for it. Jesus was appointed to be the Savior of the world, and because of this appointment God anointed Him for service.

> *Acts 10:38 — "How God anointed Jesus of Nazareth with the Holy Ghost and with power: who went about doing good, and healing all that were oppressed of the devil; for God was with him."*

When God appoints you to do something, He sends you with a word. This word is confirmed with signs and wonders following.

> *Hebrews 2:4 — "God also bearing them witness, both with signs and wonders, and with divers miracles, and gifts of the Holy Ghost, according to his own will?"*

When God sends you on a mission, He gives you a word. He then gives you His Spirit without measure to teach, enforce and transform the hearers of that word. There is no such thing as a message given by God that does not have an anointing to equip and transform the hearers of that word.

Any church service that just gives out information without transformation has only given out entertainment. Every time we attend church, we should leave with a different spiritual garment than what we came in with. In other words, we should experience the renewing of our mind. If we walk out with the same mind that we came in with, what did we come for? The altar call is not just for praying for salvation; it is for the application of the message that was preached. The altar is the place where we lay down our old way of thinking and wrestle with the angel of transformation until God has changed us.

What makes the anointing flow? EXPECTATION! Appetite must be taught. When I was born again, I had an incredible appetite for God, but there were so many things that I had no idea were available to me in the spirit. I went to a Holiness church at the time, and this radical preacher used to say, "Hold on to God until you get what you want from Him." This meant that a certain message sent from God has been preached and the windows of Heaven are open, so now wrestle with your own flesh until you move it out of the way by tarrying with God — until you get your breakthrough. "Tarrying" is an old-school term that requires determination, tenacity and hunger. You must be so hungry to receive your change that you're willing to get in God's face like there is no tomorrow. I have received breakthrough after breakthrough after learning this principle. I had no idea that God responded that way to hunger. But He loves it.

> *Hebrews 11:6 — "But without faith it is impossible to please him: for he that cometh to God must believe that he is, and that he is a rewarder of them that diligently seek him."*

How the Father Sees Me

Everything you were meant to be is what God the Father smears on you every time you come into His presence, like a shepherd rubbing oil on his sheep. Daughter, a mother never told you that you were beautiful — God says that you are the apple of His eye! Son, a father never told you that you were strong — God says that you are valiant and courageous! Every moment you spend in God's presence, He rubs your identity on you.

When you rest in the presence of God, you are entering into the Sabbath, the seventh day, the acceptable day and year of the Lord. This is the glory that Adam and Eve experienced as they fellowshipped with God in the Garden of Eden. This was the glory that was restored by our acceptance of the salvation that was paid for by Jesus Christ.

Religion has made the Sabbath into a specific day of the week, instead of realizing that it is a principle of position in relationship to God. What does it matter what day of the week we go to church? God loves us and wants us close to Him every day of the week. Does any father put legality on his children as to what days of the week they can approach him? This was only done in the Old Testament as a schoolmaster to teach Israel how to follow rules and structure. Everything in the Old Testament must be properly translated by revelation into the New Testament.

The Anointing on Your Words

Proverbs 18:21 — "Death and life are in the power of the tongue: and they that love it shall eat the fruit thereof."

One of the easiest ways to transfer the anointing that we have on us is through the spoken word. The creative power of God is released through His words. We — as sons of God, made in His image — create in the same way. Creation happens when an idea or thought comes into partnership with the spoken word. A birthing happens.

God said, "Let there be..." and there was. In Genesis we see Him creating the world in this way. Every day of our lives we are creating the exact same way. Our thoughts and beliefs are partnering with our words to create the life around us.

Some people use this power for good, but unfortunately there are some who use it for evil. There are some people who understand the way that the body, soul and spirit work, and they use words to cast spells on others for destructive purposes. These are called witches, people who use energy and words to steal, kill and destroy from others. Witches are agents of satan, and they are hidden all around us. They make our music, movies, TV shows, and they secretly affect everything around us. The manipulation of words and energy is called witchcraft. The power of witchcraft is based on manipulation, control and deception. A witch can never be more powerful than a child of God because our power is based on truth between God and His Word through relationship with Him. A witch's power is based on manipulation — but a Christian's power is based on relationship with God. The devil's power comes from our belief in his lies; therefore, the devil is empowered by those who believe in him.

The Anti-Christ

Christ: the Anointed One and His anointing
Anti-Christ: the anointing killer, the one who fights against the anointing and keeps anointed people out of anointed places

You might think that the Anti-Christ is someone outside of the Church who is fighting against the Church, but in fact it's just the opposite. The Anti-Christ spirit, in most cases, works from the inside, attempting to keep the members of the Body from working in their calling and assigned purpose.

Have you ever wondered why the Pharisees and Sadducees didn't work with Jesus but instead fought against Him? I mean, if there was someone who could walk on water, heal the sick, raise the dead and multiply food, wouldn't you want them on your team? The truth of the matter is that the anointing that was on Jesus' life pointed out the lack of anointing that was on the Pharisees and Sadducees' life. These religious leaders were part of the old wineskin, the Old Covenant of God. God was transitioning the world into a new wineskin, His New Covenant through Jesus Christ.

If you are part of an old wineskin and you discover that God is doing a new thing, you have the choice to go with the new thing or try to hold on to the old thing. People heard John the Baptist preaching, "Repent, for the Kingdom of Heaven is at hand." This means "a New Covenant is ready, so change your mind." Those who are religious will try to hold on to the past, which positions and empowers them. Those who have a relationship with God will follow the wind of the Holy Spirit wherever He is leading them.

This is what differentiates the religious from the sons of God. *"As many as are led by the Spirit of God, they are the sons of God" (Romans 8:14)*. The Pharisees and Sadducees represent the Law, and all that the Law can do is point out what's wrong with you. The Anointed One and His anointing, Jesus Christ, came to give us life — and life more abundantly. That means He had to have the ability to reverse the curses that were on mankind. He had to be empowered. He could not just come with cunning words of man's wisdom; He had to come in the demonstration and power of the Holy Spirit.

152

"Jesus Christ" effectively means "Jesus and God on Him to do those things that Jesus could not do by Himself." Jesus was and is the prototype, the grid, the example for us to follow. Each of us should be a carrier of the Christ and His anointing. Without the Christ and His anointing, we only amount to mere keepers of the Law. The Bible says, *"The letter killeth, but the Spirit giveth life" (2 Corinthians 3:6).*

Offenses

When the freedom in someone exposes the bondage in someone else, one of two things will take place. If the person who realizes that they are bound sees freedom in someone else, they then have the choice to make corrections to their own motives and behavior or to be offended. This is also how you can discern a son from an orphan.

> *Matthew 18:7 — "Woe unto the world because of offences! for it must needs be that offences come; but woe to that man by whom the offence cometh!"*

God's lie detector test: You say you are a son, huh? If you want to use God's lie detector test, just start worshipping. Freedom exposes bondage, light exposes darkness, love exposes hate, success exposes jealousy, relationship exposes religion and the Spirit of Adoption exposes the Orphan Spirit. This is why immersing yourself in worship will reveal the truth.

The Current Problem with the Church

The current state of the Church is a result of the fathers being asleep.

> *Isaiah 52:1 — "Awake, awake; put on thy strength, O Zion; put on thy beautiful garments, O Jerusalem, the holy city: for henceforth there shall no more come into thee the uncircumcised and the unclean.* ² *Shake thyself from the dust; arise, and sit down, O Jerusalem: loose thyself from the bands of thy neck, O captive daughter of Zion.* ³ *For thus saith the LORD, Ye have sold yourselves for nought; and ye shall be redeemed without money..."*

It doesn't matter if the fathers are home if they are sleeping. How many households are being run without the input, guidance or direction of a father? Yes, there is a man who lives at that address, but what good is that if he is not involved in shaping the people and vision for that home?

Key Points

1. In Adam we ALL (every human being) fell into condemnation, but in Jesus we are restored to righteousness. *(Romans 5:18-21)*
2. Jesus is the Path to Salvation. *(John 14:6)*
3. Religion and religious people are where God used to be; sons of God have a relationship with God that keeps them where God is right now. *(Romans 8:14-17)*
4. The spiritual definition of anointing means to pour on, rub into or to smear something on someone. When God anoints you, He literally puts Himself on you to

enable you to do what you were born to do. Jesus Christ, which literally means "the Anointed One and His anointing." *(Colossians 1:23)*

5. Regular time spent with God in His presence is how we keep our anointing charged up and stay full of the Holy Spirit. Getting filled with the Holy Spirit is a continual relationship and communion that we have with God. It is not a one-time filling that stays full forever. It is a relationship that must be maintained on a regular basis with God. *(1 Timothy 2:8, Isaiah 40:31)*

6. The Full Armor of God: God puts the armor on you as you wait in His presence. At the same time, the Holy Spirit is renewing your strength. *(Ephesians 6:10-18)*

7. **Gifts of the Holy Spirit** *(1 Corinthians 12:1)*:
    3 Gifts of Power
    - Faith
    - Miracles
    - Healing

    3 Gifts of Revelation
    - Words of Wisdom
    - Words of Knowledge
    - Discerning of Spirits

    3 Gifts of Inspiration
    - Prophecy
    - Tongues
    - Interpretation of Tongues

8. **What is an Anti-Christ?** – *Anti-Christ*: the anointing killer, the one who fights against the anointing and keeps anointed people out of anointed places

Notes

Notes

_____

_____

_____

_____

_____

_____

_____

_____

_____

_____

_____

_____

_____

_____

_____

_____

_____

_____

_____

_____

_____

_____

Notes

_____
_____
_____
_____
_____
_____
_____
_____
_____
_____
_____
_____
_____
_____
_____
_____
_____
_____
_____
_____
_____
_____

CHAPTER 8: THE FATHER

What a Father Does

A father must be intentional about expressing the vision for the family and helping each person under his care to develop into their individual purpose. A father needs to know the purpose for every person in his home. The father is the structure and the voice that gives guidance to keeping each person in between the lanes of their individual purpose.

Just like a driver who is heading down the road toward his destination, sometimes we get sleepy, lose focus, start coming out of our lane and consequently run into rumble strips, which immediately alert us with loud thumps that we are coming out of our lane. This is the voice of a father; this is the discipline that a father has taught you that is built into your personality. A father says the same thing over and over again until it becomes engraved in your soul. A father is a person who establishes the lines in your soul in the same way that a farmer establishes lines on his farm. The lines on a farm provide organization and discipline to the field, allowing structured growth, watering, cultivation and harvest.

Without healthy structure and guidance, the result most likely will be a container with unforeseen weaknesses, full of parts that are out of place. That's like sending a kid to go get two bags of groceries from the store and giving them a wet paper bag to put them in. It's inevitable that before they get home, groceries will be all over the street. What happens when you don't prepare a human being for life and you send them out of your house at 18 or earlier when you haven't prepared the container, the vessel and the soul to successfully navigate life? There is no coincidence who your dad was or wasn't, whether he was there or not. Every child was entrusted to a parent for a reason because of what that father would or would not deposit into them. If your father was not there, life did not mean for you to live with a shortage... there will be someone who shows up to give you the guidance that you need. It may start in a book, a mentor, a sports program with a coach, or some other way. The main point is that life is always unfolding and bringing you exactly where you are supposed to be.

Where are the fathers? I looked at the church and I see kids running around everywhere. Kids with no manners, kids with no discipline, kids with no fathers. Yes, there is a person preaching and he is in charge of the church, but he has not taken the responsibility for those children. When you have the heart of the Father and you look at people, you want God's best for them. When you have the Father's heart, it possesses you, leads you and guides you to shape those who are around you. When God highlights a spiritual son to a spiritual father, it is just as though that person becomes your son. For three and a half years, the 12 disciples walked in the identity of Jesus' spiritual sons.

In *John 17*, as Jesus is about to be crucified and go back to the Father, you see the heart that Jesus has for the Father and that the Father has for His Son. Then you get the revelation that Jesus is praying for those disciples who have been His spiritual sons for three and a half years. Jesus did not pray for the disciples like He was praying for strangers who came to a church service, as though they were only under His care for a few hours. He prayed for these disciples like His life depended on it, realizing that God had entrusted these men to His care.

Jesus was preparing these sons to be glorified even as He was glorified. Jesus was teaching these sons how to believe, and because of the belief that Jesus taught them and the words of God that Jesus received and then passed on to them, the disciples were put in a position to receive the Glory of God. So then, Jesus was able to pray to the Father and say, "Glorify them even as You have glorified me."

So, when you look at the church and wonder what's missing — when you look at Christians and wonder why they can't do what Jesus did — it is because we are missing the main ingredient of what Jesus had and what Jesus was praying for the disciples to receive: the Glory of God.

The tragedy of any church is to operate as though the Glory of God is there when in reality it is *not*. The Bible calls us "Kings and Priests unto God." Kings have the authority and Priests have the access to the Glory of God. But both Kings and Priests know that there is a protocol and that you cannot come before the King and before God just any kind of way.

This is where we have the opportunity to hit the mark or to miss it in church. The leader of the service must operate according to God's protocol and not according to the protocol of men. The leader of the service must always have in mind what God wants, what God requires and what God is asking for in the moment. What God asked for in the last service may not be what God is asking for in today's service. The key is not to try to regulate God down to a formula but to know Him through relationship and be sensitive enough to follow the leading of the Holy Spirit, who will lead us directly into the Glory if we are willing to follow Him. Practicing the presence of God is an art that must become a mastery to a son of God. The heart that is in tune with the Holy Spirit is what leads us into the presence of God.

One day, we will arrive in Heaven and have the full awareness that the greatest Teacher who ever existed was living inside of us the whole time we were on earth. We will be embarrassed at what questions we could have asked Him but did not. The greatest power that ever existed lives on the inside of us, waiting to be accessed at any moment. The greatest Friend, Teacher, Mentor, Trainer and Instructor that we could ever find is waiting 24 hours of the day to talk to us. The only thing that could keep us away from the Glory of God is ourselves... our motives, our intentions, our religiosity and our lack of willingness to be led.

What Made Jesus a Son

We are now in the season where we have the opportunity to return to the Glory of God. He is waiting right where we left Him: in a place of obedience, in a place of fellowship and in a place of sonship. When we look at Jesus, we must realize that it was His heart that made Him a Son.

If you look at any great individual in the Bible, study any great revival in history or look at any great move of God, you will find a man or woman who has learned how to practice the presence of God. For a son of God, the presence of God supersedes doctrine, theology or any ceremonialism that we could come up with. Who cares if we have a service, if God didn't show up because we didn't give Him what He asked for? A church service is not successful just because it takes up a big offering, has a large number in attendance or a stage full of performers. A successful church service is a service where the Holy Spirit approves and confirms your sacrifice by releasing the Glory of God to let you know that you just created the atmosphere of Heaven with your obedience.

So, we should ask ourselves, "What have we been trading in the Glory of God for?"

Right Now

We often think that our change, deliverance or freedom is far away — when actually it is only one decision away. Change seems so hard for us because we look at it through the scope of how much time it's going to take for me to get to this change, as though we are driving several miles away to a destination.

In Kingdom reality, change is only one lane away. When you change your clothes, you don't think your next change is miles away, for it's only moments away. And that's why when Jesus came on the scene, He said, "Repent, for the Kingdom of Heaven is at hand." That means a new lane has been opened. The Old Testament was the old lane, so when Jesus said, "Repent," He was saying, "Switch lanes." Hey Jesus, how long does it take for us to get from the Old Testament to the New Testament? Jesus replies, "It's just the next lane over!"

Repent is not a religious word; it just means to change your mind. This is a HUGE revelation that removes the stress, pressure and anxiety of feeling like you are responsible for obtaining your own change. When, in reality, as soon as you make that decision, the provision that you need is now available.

So now, wherever there is pride, humility is just in the other lane. Wherever there is discouragement, expectation is in the other lane. Wherever there is hatred, love and compassion are in the other lane. There is now always another lane available waiting for your decision! It's not later on — **it's right now!**

What God Gives You

God will only accept what He asks you for. This is the difference between your offering being accepted or not accepted, being a son or being an orphan. The key to this is that an orphan is going to do things his way no matter what you tell him to do. On the other hand, a son always desires to be obedient, compliant and pleasing to his Father without delay.

God has simplified the process of prayer by giving us the answers and asking us to simply give Him back what He gave us. This requires us to have a listening ear that is poised to hear the voice of the Holy Spirit. The major key to prayer is praying the words and Scriptures that the Holy

Spirit is giving you in the moment. This is called the *Rhema* word of God.

Ask yourself what is more important: what you said or what you are saying right now? This is the key to relationship, because anyone can open the Bible and read to you what God said, but only someone who is in a current relationship with God can hear the right-now, *Rhema* voice of God. God wants us to pull down His glory in fellowship with Him so that we can give back what He has given us.

> *John 17:1 — "These words spake Jesus, and lifted up his eyes to heaven, and said, Father, the hour is come; glorify thy Son, that thy Son also may glorify thee: ² As thou hast given him power over all flesh, that he should give eternal life to as many as thou hast given him. ³ And this is life eternal, that they might know thee the only true God, and Jesus Christ, whom thou hast sent. ⁴ I have glorified thee on the earth: I have finished the work which thou gavest me to do. ⁵ And now, O Father, glorify thou me with thine own self with the glory which I had with thee before the world was. ⁶ I have manifested thy name unto the men which thou gavest me out of the world: thine they were, and thou gavest them me; and they have kept thy word."*

Jesus modeled to the disciples the perfect way for a son to pray. A son makes a request to God when he sees anything on the earth that does not align with God's will in Heaven. Heaven now has permission to complete the transaction and bring down God's will on earth as it is in Heaven. Angels are assigned to us to help us accomplish our purpose in this life. They are looking for God's words to come out of our mouths so that our prayers can be answered according to God's will.

John 17:7 —"Now they have known that all things whatsoever thou hast given me are of thee. ⁸ For I have given unto them the words which thou gavest me; and they have received them, and have known surely that I came out from thee, and they have believed that thou didst send me. ⁹ I pray for them: I pray not for the world, but for them which thou hast given me; for they are thine. ¹⁰ And all mine are thine, and thine are mine; and I am glorified in them. ¹¹ And now I am no more in the world, but these are in the world, and I come to thee. Holy Father, keep through thine own name those whom thou hast given me, that they may be one, as we are. ¹² While I was with them in the world, I kept them in thy name: those that thou gavest me I have kept, and none of them is lost, but the son of perdition; that the scripture might be fulfilled. ¹³ And now come I to thee; and these things I speak in the world, that they might have my joy fulfilled in themselves."

To make a long story short, God wants us to give Him back exactly what He gives to us. When God wants to deposit something into the earth, He gives you a word. He speaks that word directly into your spirit, and then you speak out and declare that word into existence. The angels see the Word of God, which was spoken by God, now being spoken by us, and a heavenly transaction has been made because we have come into covenant agreement and alignment with God. Heaven now has permission to complete the transaction to bring God's will on earth.

The Restoration to the Father

The Kingdom of God is the family of God. Jesus did not die just to pay for our sins; He died because we had been sold into orphan hood by Adam and Eve. Through their rebellious act we all lost our position as heirs of this world, called by inheritance to take dominion of the earth and to subdue it. We lost our home in the Garden of Eden, which represented the Kingdom of God on earth. Last but not least, we lost the Glory of God that had clothed Adam and Eve because of the proximity of their relationship to the Father (as mentioned before). The enemy of mankind had one objective in His discussion with Eve in the Garden, and it was to cause her through doubt and unbelief to be separated from the Father. Her disobedience, joined with Adam's agreement to willingly disobey God the Father, catapulting them from the light into darkness, from fellowship and Holy Communion into exile, and ultimately from the Law of life wrapped in the Glory of God into the Law of sin and death.

So, this is the reason for the celebration when Jesus was born. The angels knew that the Savior of the world was here, and now the way would be made for mankind to be rejoined with God the Father.

There is no Kingdom without God the Father. Jesus stated numerous times that everything the Father had was His, and everything He did as the Son of God was as a result of what the Father showed Him to do *(John 5:19; 8:29; 16:15)*. When you are saved through repentance of sins and washed in the blood of Jesus, you are born again. You have come from death into life, and your name is placed in the Lamb's book of life *(Luke 10:20; Philippians 4:3)*. Then you have the opportunity to celebrate an open show of your conversion by being water baptized *(1 Peter 3:21; Acts 10:48)*. Finally, you pray for the infilling of the Holy Spirit, to be endued with power *(Acts 1:8; Luke 24:49)*.

Malachi 4:6 — "And he shall turn the heart of the fathers to the children, and the heart of the children to their fathers, lest I come and smite the earth with a curse."

If you look at the state of the world, you can describe it in just one word: fatherless! This is not because God the Father is not there but because the world as a whole has turned its back on Him. This puts mankind in position for the greatest revival that this world has ever seen — a revival that will cause leaders to rise up who have the heart of God the Father. Having the Father's heart will allow us to model Jesus and raise up the sons of God that creation is groaning for *(Romans 8:22)*. A glorious time and season is upon us, and it will look like the greatest revival that the world has ever seen.

In order to revive something, it either has to be dead or in the process of dying. So, why do we use the term "revival"? Jesus IS Revival! Jesus is the restoration and definition of everything that a son is supposed to be. Jesus is the example of God's original intent for mankind. Jesus is the example of mankind operating in the fullness of its potential.

Colossians 2:9 — "For in him dwelleth all the fulness of the Godhead bodily. ¹⁰ And ye are complete in him, which is the head of all principality and power... ¹³ And you, being dead in your sins and the uncircumcision of your flesh, hath he quickened together with him, having forgiven you all trespasses."

So, if you were wondering what revival looks like, look at Jesus. Jesus showed the disciples for three and a half years what revival looked like. He modeled revival. Jesus was revival on legs, walking anywhere God wanted to reveal Him. The Kingdom of God is revival. If what we are doing feels like a dead, dry branch disconnected from the vine, we are not in Him. And if we are not in Him, then we are not in revival! And if we are not in Christ, then we are not operating in the newness of life that was made available for us.

> *2 Corinthians 5:17 — "Therefore if any man be in Christ, he is a new creature: old things are passed away; behold, all things are become new. [18] And all things are of God, who hath reconciled us to himself by Jesus Christ, and hath given to us the ministry of reconciliation; [19] To wit, that God was in Christ, reconciling the world unto himself, not imputing their trespasses unto them; and hath committed unto us the word of reconciliation."*

The True Sinners

It wasn't the people whose sin you could see but the people whose sin you couldn't see that was the problem. The Sadducees, Pharisees, Chief Priests, Lawyers, Rulers and Judges were the keepers of the Law, and they were in charge of the Church at that time. When Jesus came on the scene, He brought the truth. But they wanted "church"! They wanted religion! They wanted their denominations! And all these things were more important to them than the truth. The Truth (Jesus) was healing the sick, raising the dead and making blind eyes to see, but to these religious men, the Law was more attractive. Life was right in front of them, but instead they would choose the Law that bound them to death because of their sins.

Jesus never had a fight with sinners; they never disputed who He was or what He was called to do. The true definition of sin is the thoughts that separate us from God. You would think it was the actions that we do, but they are just the fruit that are a result of the root of our thinking.

As God positions us for the end-time Revival that will change the world, keep your eyes open for the same spirits that fought against Jesus to fight against revival. The Sadducees, Pharisees, Chief Priests, Lawyers, Rulers and Judges represent Anti-Christ spirits that live in the Church and have their own motives and intentions. We would all like to think that everyone in the Church has pure motives and intentions toward God and His will, but they don't. There are many people in church for a position, prestige, power or a paycheck. We have learned through many trials and tribulations that the parables of the wheat and the tares and of the sheep and the goats are real.

There are some things to keep an eye out for that will help identify the imposters:

1. Motives – If our motives are not Kingdom-centered and driven by love, then what are they?
2. Love – The never-failing love that we see described in *1 Corinthians 13* is undeniable.
3. Fruit – You will know a tree by the fruit it bears. *(Matthew 7:15-17)*

Why is this important? Because when Jesus brought revival, there were enemies positioned to stop it. So we must be ready to contend earnestly for the faith that is delivered to us. We must "put on the full armor of God so that we will be able to stand in the evil day, and having done all, to stand" *(Ephesians 6:13-17)*. No doubt about it, we are in a war... not with sinners or even with the world, but with Religion. It's important to know that, so that you know exactly where the enemy will come from. The true sinners are those who use the Church and Word of God to lead people astray. They are doing spiritual things without the Holy Spirit — in the flesh — opening doors that Paul called "doctrines of devils."

> *1 Timothy 4:1 — "Now the Spirit speaketh expressly, that in the latter times some shall depart from the faith, giving heed to seducing spirits, and doctrines of devils; ² Speaking lies in hypocrisy; having their conscience seared with a hot iron."*

Sons will always expose snakes. One of the first things that Moses had to fight were the snakes of the Egyptian Pharaoh's magicians. Jealousy, envy, strife and every evil workflow out of the heart of those who are falsely motivated and led by their flesh *(James 3:16)*. We are putting this part in the book because it is often alarming for anointed people to face adversity from those who should honor and support them. Don't be discouraged when you are marching toward your goal for God and you are not celebrated. Your motives and intentions must also be purified. In the end, whatever we do must be for God and come fully out of our love for Him.

A Glorious Church

A glorious Church is rising up, prepared by Jesus, without spot or wrinkle!

> *Ephesians 5:27 — "That he might present it to himself a glorious church, not having spot, or wrinkle, or any such thing; but that it should be holy and without blemish."*

This Church will be full of sons and daughters who have been reconnected with the Father and are walking in their full Kingdom identity. These are sons who love the Father and have the mind frame to do those things that are

171

pleasing in His sight *(John 8:28-29)*. God is looking for sons and daughters who will carry out the Kingdom every day — those who will love one another as they love themselves and who are led by the Spirit of God above all things. This is the time when the Glory of God is going to be shown through those who have come to know Jesus as "the Way" and have been reconciled, having become one with the Father. The Father seeks those who He can show Himself strong in.

Salvation with Jesus, Communion with Holy Spirit and Oneness with the Father

Until this time, we have thought that the mission of Jesus was just to bring us to Salvation and buy us a ticket off of earth and into Heaven. Then we received a deeper revelation of the life that could be lived as we were filled with the Holy Spirit. Now we would like to submit to you the revelation that Jesus was relaying to His disciples as He was preparing to leave earth and be crucified. In the verses below are the key to doing the things that Jesus did — and greater:

> *John 14:10 — "Believest thou not that I am in the Father, and the Father in me? the words that I speak unto you I speak not of myself: but the Father that dwelleth in me, he doeth the works. ¹¹ Believe me that I am in the Father, and the Father in me: or else believe me for the very works' sake. ¹² Verily, verily, I say unto you, He that believeth on me, the works that I do shall he do also; and greater works than these shall he do; because I go unto my Father. ¹³ And whatsoever ye shall ask in my name, that will I do, that the Father may be glorified in the Son. ¹⁴ If ye shall ask any thing in my name, I will do it."*

The key to doing the things that Jesus did is revealed as you pay attention to what Jesus kept saying over and over again: "I am in the Father and the Father is in me." We are taught to pray for Salvation and then to be filled with the Holy Spirit, but Jesus also said that He would bring the Father back to live inside of us and make Their abode in us.

John 14:23 — "Jesus answered and said unto him, If a man love me, he will keep my words: and my Father will love him, and we will come unto him, and make our abode with him."

Jesus' mission was to bring us back into fellowship with the Father so that He could live on the inside of us and we could become one. Salvation was never intended to rescue us from earth but to transform us into sons of God who would take dominion over the earth and every other planet that God would give us dominion over. We are destined to rule over planets and galaxies as the sons of God who have learned to follow the voice, Word and divine Spirit of God. When we rule over the world to come, we will be able to say like Jesus did, "If you have seen me, you have seen the Father!" *(John 14:9)*.

When you only understand part of the journey, then there's no way that you can make it to your destination. We were told that Jesus was the end destination, but in reality the Father is. If you only made it to Jesus, then you only made it part of the way.

The Way God Does Things

The Bible says, "Without a vision, people perish" *(Proverbs 29:18)*. But the next thing you need to know is who God gives the vision to, because contrary to popular belief, it does matter how things are built in the Kingdom of God.

> *1 Corinthians 14:40 — "Let all things be done decently and in order."*

> *Psalm 127:1 — "Except the Lord build the house, they labour in vain that build it: except the Lord keep the city, the watchman waketh but in vain."*

> *Ephesians 4:11 — "And he gave some, apostles; and some, prophets; and some, evangelists; and some, pastors and teachers; ^{12} For the perfecting of the saints, for the work of the ministry, for the edifying of the body of Christ: ^{13} Till we all come in the unity of the faith, and of the knowledge of the Son of God, unto a perfect man, unto the measure of the stature of the fulness of Christ: ^{14} That we henceforth be no more children, tossed to and fro, and carried about with every wind of doctrine, by the sleight of men, and cunning craftiness, whereby they lie in wait to deceive; ^{15} But speaking the truth in love, may grow up into him in all things, which is the head, even Christ: ^{16} From whom the whole body fitly joined together and compacted by that which every joint supplieth, according to the effectual working in the measure of every part, maketh increase of the body unto the edifying of itself in love."*

From these verses you can draw out the conclusion that it is absolutely necessary to build with God and it is impossible to build what God wants correctly without Him. If we build without Him, the result will be a religious organization, built upon religious laws and dogma, led by the flesh and "the letter that kills," and void of Holy Spirit supernatural power. Now this is when things get dangerous. If we do spiritual things without the Holy Spirit, we are opening the door for another spirit to come in and fill that space because we are not submitted to God's Spirit. *James 4:7* says, *"Submit yourselves therefore to God. Resist the devil, and he will flee from you."*

So, when we choose not to be Holy Spirit led, our churches get filled with familiar spirits that act religious but have no positive spiritual value. Instead, those spirits steal from, kill and destroy the Body of Christ from within. The sheep then are ever learning but never coming to the knowledge of the truth in God's Word. No Truth means no Revelation. No Revelation means no Transformation. And no Transformation means no Elevation up the mountain of relationship with God, where we receive the prize of sonship, Transfiguration *(Matthew 17)*.

Our goal is always to build with Holy Spirit! He is the best at everything, and He knows how to do everything that God has called us to do. The thing about being a son is that the position is in direct connection to the Father. There is no son without the Father, because everything that Jesus had or did came from the Father. Check out this passage in John 5:

> *John 5:18 — "Therefore the Jews sought the more to kill him, because he not only had broken the sabbath, but said also that God was his Father, making himself equal with God. [19] Then answered Jesus and said unto them, Verily, verily, I say unto you, The Son can do nothing of himself, but what he seeth the Father do: for what things soever he doeth, these also doeth the Son likewise. [20] For the Father loveth the Son, and sheweth him all things that himself doeth: and he will shew him greater works than these, that ye may marvel. [21] For as the Father raiseth up the dead, and quickeneth them; even so the Son quickeneth whom he will. [22] For the Father judgeth no man, but hath committed all judgment unto the Son: [23] That all men should honour*

the Son, even as they honour the Father. He that honoureth not the Son honoureth not the Father which hath sent him."

The Gospel of Reconciliation

As Jesus starts speaking in **John 16:23,** He begins to prophesy about a specific time and season. Marked by a "verily, verily" ("pay attention, pay attention"), Jesus describes a time when because we love Jesus and believe that Jesus came out from God, we now have direct access to God the Father to ask for anything in Jesus' name, and He will do it.

John 16:23 — "And in that day ye shall ask me nothing. Verily, verily, I say unto you, Whatsoever ye shall ask the Father in my name, he will give it you. [24] Hitherto have ye asked nothing in my name: ask, and ye shall receive, that your joy may be full. [25] These things have I spoken unto you in proverbs: but the time cometh, when I shall no more speak unto you in proverbs, but I shall shew you plainly of the Father. [26] At that day ye shall ask in my name: and I say not unto you, that I will pray the Father for you: [27] For the Father himself loveth you, because ye have loved me, and have believed that I came out from God. [28] I came forth from the Father, and am come into the world: again, I leave the world, and go to the Father."

You may be saying to yourself, "I have had this access to God the Father ever since I prayed for Salvation and accepted Jesus as my personal Lord and Savior, right?" My answer to that statement would be "in principal, yes; in the spirit, yes; seated in heavenly places in Christ Jesus, yes." But according to *1 Corinthians 13*, sonship is something that we grow into, and when we become men, we put away childish things, meaning a childish understanding about God, because up until graduation day, we only knew Him in part.

> *1 Corinthians 13:12 — "For now we see through a glass, darkly; but then face to face: now I know in part; but then shall I know even as also I am known"*

In the absence of spiritual fathers and proper understanding of the Scriptures, we have assumed that the prayer of Salvation was a finished destination, when it was actually just qualification and registration for the race. To put it in other words, we have assumed or most often been misinformed that everything in Salvation is ours by Grace, when actually it must be obtained by finishing our race. *Matthew 24:13* speaks of what the end times will be like and adds, *"But he that shall endure unto the end, the same shall be saved."* Does the prayer of repentance and confession in Jesus as Lord and Savior qualify us for Salvation and Heaven? Yes. But the journey is not yet over, so keep walking with Jesus and allow Him to take you from bystander to servant, and from servant to son.

The Key Is Enduring to the End

If Salvation is presented to us correctly, it will be presented as a race and not a finish line where we wait for Jesus to whisk us away into Heaven. God did not send Jesus to rescue us from this world and bring us to Heaven because things are just so terrible here on earth. God the Father sent His only begotten Son to be the offering to pay for the offense that separated mankind from Him through Adam and Eve's transgression. After receiving Salvation, we are now registered for the greatest race this world has ever seen. It is the race for sonship, or better defined as Transfiguration.

> *Hebrews 3:6 — "But Christ as a son over his own house; whose house are we, if we hold fast the confidence and the rejoicing of the hope firm unto the end."*

Just as in *1 Corinthians 13*, *1 John 3* speaks of an ongoing transformation or transaction that is happening inside of us.

> *1 John 3:1 — "Behold, what manner of love the Father hath bestowed upon us, that we should be called the sons of God: therefore the world knoweth us not, because it knew him not. ² Beloved, now are we the sons of God, and it doth not yet appear what we shall be: but we know that, when he shall appear, we shall be like him; for we shall see him as he is."*

We are described in 1 Corinthians 13 as just having pieces of the image of Jesus, knowing Him only in part. In verse 9 and 10 of the same chapter, it reads, *"For we know in part, and we prophesy in part. But when that which is perfect is come, then that which is in part shall be done away."*

A good way for us to understand the concept of sonship that must be walked out over time is by looking at the concepts listed below.

A military enlistee signs a contract, says an oath, and now he or she is qualified to become a soldier. From the moment the enlistee signs the contract, raise their hand and affirm the oath, they are already considered to be in the military, but it is not fully certified until after training.

A man and a woman have a baby together; the man becomes a father and the woman becomes a mother. But the act of being a mother or a father is something that is learned, developed and fleshed out over time.

A man and a woman get married, as they have signed a wedding contract and celebrated their union with a ceremony that announces their decision. They have both filled the position, which is no longer open, but the journey to becoming a husband or wife has just begun.

The Bible calls us the bride of Christ, and it says that Jesus is going to prepare us to be a Bride without spots or wrinkles. This means that we are currently in a state of development as the bride of Christ.

> *Ephesians 5:25 — "Husbands, love your wives, even as Christ also loved the church, and gave himself for it;* [26] *That he might sanctify and cleanse it with the washing of water by the word,* [27] *That he might present it to himself a glorious church, not having spot, or wrinkle, or any such thing; but that it should be holy and without blemish."*

Still in the Process

The problem is when we pretend to be a finished or completed work while we are still in the process. God adopts us into His family, and then we get to grow into becoming sons. It is not an instant transaction but one that is cultivated and monitored by the Holy Spirit. The Bible often declares things over us that must be walked into, just like the Promised Land. Being chosen by God, Israel was already qualified for their God-given inheritance of the Promised Land. Unfortunately, the hearts of all the people were not with God. They had been delivered out of the captivity of Egypt by God's mighty hand and with signs and wonders. They had also been processed by God for over 40 years, tested and tried. God's diagnosis of Israel reads like this:

> *Deuteronomy 8:2 — "And thou shalt remember all the way which the LORD thy God led thee these forty years in the wilderness, to humble thee, and to prove thee, to know what was in thine heart, whether thou wouldest keep his commandments, or no. ³ And he humbled thee, and suffered thee to hunger, and fed thee with manna, which thou knewest not, neither did thy fathers know; that he might make thee know that man doth not live by bread only, but by every word that proceedeth out of the mouth of the LORD doth man live. ⁴ Thy raiment waxed not old upon thee, neither did thy foot swell, these forty years. ⁵ Thou shalt also consider in thine heart, that, as a man chasteneth his son, so the LORD thy God chasteneth thee."*

The Battle Is in the Soul

So, God brought a people called Israel out of Egypt, taking them through the wilderness of processing to a place where they could inherit the Promised Land that He had prepared for them. So, what stopped them? Let's see what Moses said about them in Deuteronomy 9:

> *Deuteronomy 9:6 — "Understand therefore, that the LORD thy God giveth thee not this good land to possess it for thy righteousness; for thou art a stiffnecked people. ⁷ Remember, and forget not, how thou provokedst the LORD thy God to wrath in the wilderness: from the day that thou didst depart out of the land of Egypt, until ye came unto this place, ye have been rebellious against the LORD. ⁸ Also in Horeb ye provoked the LORD to wrath, so that the LORD was angry with you to have destroyed you. ⁹ When I was*

gone up into the mount to receive the tables of stone, even the tables of the covenant which the LORD made with you, then I abode in the mount forty days and forty nights, I neither did eat bread nor drink water: ¹⁰ And the LORD delivered unto me two tables of stone written with the finger of God; and on them was written according to all the words, which the LORD spake with you in the mount out of the midst of the fire in the day of the assembly. ¹¹ And it came to pass at the end of forty days and forty nights, that the LORD gave me the two tables of stone, even the tables of the covenant. ¹² And the LORD said unto me, Arise, get thee down quickly from hence; for thy people which thou hast brought forth out of Egypt have corrupted themselves; they are quickly turned aside out of the way which I commanded them; they have made them a molten image. ¹³ Furthermore the LORD spake unto me, saying, I have seen this people, and, behold, it is a stiffnecked people: ¹⁴ Let me alone, that I may destroy them, and blot out their name from under heaven: and I will make of thee a nation mightier and greater than they."

Pay attention to the language of Moses as he describes the hearts of the Israelites. The people of Israel represent a principle that we all embody until we truly surrender ourselves to God, and that is REBELLION. Our hearts are what God is looking at when He deals with us. How do we respond to His Word? How do we respond to His voice? How do we respond to the things that God has done in our lives? All these things are important to God, and you'd better believe that God is keeping a detailed record of His dealings with us. Let's read further into this history lesson by Moses:

Deuteronomy 9:15 — "So I turned and came down from the mount, and the mount burned with fire: and the two tables of the covenant were in my two hands. ¹⁶ And I looked, and, behold, ye had sinned against the LORD your God, and had made you a molten calf: ye had turned aside quickly out of the way which the LORD had commanded you. ¹⁷ And I took the two tables, and cast them out of my two hands, and brake them before your eyes. ¹⁸ And I fell down before the LORD, as at the first, forty days and forty nights: I did neither eat bread, nor drink water, because of all your sins which ye sinned, in doing wickedly in the sight of the LORD, to provoke him to anger. ¹⁹ For I was afraid of the anger and hot displeasure, wherewith the LORD was wroth against you to destroy you. But the LORD hearkened unto me at that time also. ²⁰ And the LORD was very angry with Aaron to have destroyed him: and I prayed for Aaron also the same time. ²¹ And I took your sin, the calf which ye had made, and burnt it with fire, and stamped it, and ground it very small, even until it was as small as dust: and I cast the dust thereof into the brook that descended out of the mount."

When we consider the patience of Moses to deal with such a rebellious and stiff-necked people, his task was extraordinary. I mean, a pastor reading this story may have one, two or even three church events a week where they interact with a congregation for a few hours. Moses had to deal with over 2 million Israelites *day and night* from the moment he brought them out of Egypt. Moses goes on to remind the Israelites of just how faithful God has been to the promises that He made to Abraham, Isaac and Jacob, their forefathers.

Deuteronomy 9:22 — "And at Taberah, and at Massah, and at Kibrothhattaavah, ye provoked the LORD to wrath. ²³ Likewise when the LORD sent you from Kadeshbarnea, saying, Go up and possess the land which I have given you; then ye rebelled against the commandment of the LORD your God, and ye believed him not, nor hearkened to his voice. [24] Ye have been rebellious against the LORD from the day that I knew you. [25] Thus I fell down before the LORD forty days and forty nights, as I fell down at the first; because the LORD had said he would destroy you. [26] I prayed therefore unto the LORD, and said, O Lord GOD, destroy not thy people and thine inheritance, which thou hast redeemed through thy greatness, which thou hast brought forth out of Egypt with a mighty hand. [27] Remember thy servants, Abraham, Isaac, and Jacob; look not unto the stubbornness of this people, nor to their wickedness, nor to their sin: [28] Lest the land whence thou broughtest us out say, Because the LORD was not able to bring them into the land which he promised them, and because he hated them, he hath brought them out to slay them in the wilderness. [29] Yet they are thy people and thine inheritance, which thou broughtest out by thy mighty power and by thy stretched out arm."

In the course of these passages, Moses has had three fasts lasting 40 days and 40 nights, without food or water, all for the sake of the children of Israel. That's an incredible feat of love and leadership displayed by Moses as he is tried by God. God even offered to destroy the Israelites on multiple occasions, stating that He could make Moses another "nation of people who would be mightier and greater" (verses 13 to 14). In that same set of verses, God offered to "blot out the children of Israel's name from under Heaven."

God called the children of Israel stiff-necked, and Moses summed it up by saying that they had been rebellious against God from the moment He met them (verse 24). The key to their heart posture was the same key that made mankind walk away from God the Father in the first place: Rebellion! The adversary, satan, tricked Adam and Eve by getting them to surrender their identity to him. He made them think that God was keeping something from them, and he offered them the same curse of rebellion that he himself had entered into as he separated himself from God the Father *(Ezekiel 28; Isaiah 14)*. The devil, having no new tricks, tried the same thing on Jesus after His 40-day fast and trip into the wilderness *(Matthew 4:1)*.

The Mountain of Transfiguration

What is our goal? How will we know when we have passed the son test and that we have passed from being *qualified* to enter the race to being *verified* by Abba Father, Daddy God Himself? We spoke about these verses earlier, but we would like to highlight a few points that merit repeating:

> *Matthew 17:1 — "And after six days Jesus taketh Peter, James, and John his brother, and bringeth them up into an high mountain apart, ²And was transfigured before them: and his face did shine as the sun, and his raiment was white as the light. ³And, behold, there appeared unto them Moses and Elias talking with him. ⁴Then answered Peter, and said unto Jesus, Lord, it is good for us to be here: if thou wilt, let us make here three tabernacles; one for thee, and one for Moses, and one for Elias. ⁵While he yet spake, behold, a bright cloud overshadowed them: and behold a voice out of the cloud, which said, This is my beloved Son, in whom I am well pleased; hear ye him."*

Two times God shows up in the Bible to honor Jesus' progress, first at His baptism in the Jordan with John, and the second time on the mountain of Transfiguration. On this mountain, two special guests show up to the ceremony, and Jesus is magnificently transfigured before them.

> *Matthew 17:6 — "And when the disciples heard it, they fell on their face, and were sore afraid. [7] And Jesus came and touched them, and said, Arise, and be not afraid. [8] And when they had lifted up their eyes, they saw no man, save Jesus only. [9] And as they came down from the mountain, Jesus charged them, saying, Tell the vision to no man, until the Son of man be risen again from the dead. [10] And his disciples asked him, saying, Why then say the scribes that Elias must first come? [11] And Jesus answered and said unto them, Elias truly shall first come, and restore all things."*

Another key revelation tucked into verses 10 and 11 is a prophetic message of a man coming in the spirit of Elias (Elijah) who must come first in the last days.

> *Malachi 4:5 — "Behold, I will send you Elijah the prophet before the coming of the great and dreadful day of the LORD: [6] And he shall turn the heart of the fathers to the children, and the heart of the children to their fathers, lest I come and smite the earth with a curse."*

Jesus our Savior is our example and the perfect benchmark for sonship. When we can do those things that Jesus did and greater, then we can say that we are walking in the footsteps of our big Brother, Lord and Savior.

> *2 Peter 1:17 — "For he received from God the Father honour and glory, when there came such a voice to him from the excellent glory, This is my beloved Son, in whom I am well pleased."*

John 14:9 — "Jesus saith unto him, Have I been so long time with you, and yet hast thou not known me, Philip? he that hath seen me hath seen the Father; and how sayest thou then, Show us the Father? ¹⁰ Believest thou not that I am in the Father, and the Father in me? the words that I speak unto you I speak not of myself: but the Father that dwelleth in me, he doeth the works. ¹¹ Believe me that I am in the Father, and the Father in me: or else believe me for the very works' sake. ¹² Verily, verily, I say unto you, He that believeth on me, the works that I do shall he do also; and greater works than these shall he do; because I go unto my Father. ¹³ And whatsoever ye shall ask in my name, that will I do, that the Father may be glorified in the Son."

The Characteristics of Fatherlessness
- Rebellion
- Narcissism
- Arrogance
- Poor Self-Image
- Low Self-Esteem
- Selfishness
- Lack of Confidence
- Pride
- Covetousness
- Disobedience
- Boasting
- Blasphemy
- Ungratefulness
- Greed

The Characteristics of Sonship
- Relationship with God the Father
- Guidance
- Obedience

> Repentance (exchange of thoughts)
> Healing
> Reconciliation
> Identity
> Selflessness
> Confidence
> Humility
> Giving
> Self-control
> Gratefulness
> Purpose

Action Steps for Restoring the Father
1. **The Body of Christ**: It is essential to get plugged into a church that is led by a father who is connected to the Father heart of God and who is led by the Holy Spirit. A Holy Spirit-led leader with the Father's heart will help you grow into your purpose as you walk toward your destiny.

2. **Finding Mentors** (accountability partners): Get connected to Kingdom family that you can walk out your life with God with. This should only be a few essential people who God has specifically placed in your life to develop the core essence of who you are. These are the people who you share your intimate struggles and victories with, those who have spent the necessary time to get to know when you are behaving as yourself or when you are acting out of character. There are essential vitamins and protection that come from having a core group to keep you accountable.

3. **Books and Self-Developing Materials**: Staying in a place of learning brings new information to you. The more information you are filled with, the more God

can use it to make principal connections, bring awareness to your personal challenges or even bring a new perspective on a subject. All information that we consume should be regulated by the Holy Spirit.

4. **Counseling/Group Discussions**: Finding a safe environment that enables you to flush out your thoughts is very important when it comes to renewing your mind. Sometimes we don't know how "in or out of alignment" our thoughts are until we get around others who may challenge them.

5. **Declarations**: Biblical declarations change the atmosphere around you. Repetition is needed in order to change the programming inside of us. We as humans will repeat the same actions over and over again unless our programming is changed through mind-renewing declarations.

6. **Meditations**: This means to meditate on the Word of God day and night until it begins to produce fruit in your soul. This also means to meditate on your future goals, ambitions and accomplishments to come. Meditation brings revelation, revelation promotes correlation and correlation leads to elevation in your thoughts and ways of thinking.

7. **Practicing the Presence of God**: Nobody gets you ready for becoming a son of God like the Holy Spirit. He is EVERYTHING! He is our Comforter, Guide, Teacher, Life Coach and overall Best Friend. He loves us intimately and is waiting to teach us everything that we need to know to make us a full-fledged son of God. He does not speak of Himself, but He takes the things that belong to Jesus and reveals them to us *(John 16:13)*.

Key Points

1. A father is a person who establishes the lines in your soul in the same way that a farmer establishes lines on his farm. The lines in a farm provide organization and discipline to the field, allowing structured growth, watering, cultivation, and harvest.

2. In Kingdom reality, change is only one lane away. When Jesus came on the scene, He said, "Repent, for the Kingdom of Heaven is at hand." That means a new lane has been opened. The Old Testament was the old lane, so when Jesus said, "Repent," He was saying, "Switch lanes." *(Matthew 4:17)*

3. *Repent* is not a religious word; it just means to change your mind. As soon as you make that decision, the provision that you need is now available. *(Acts 3:19)*

4. There is no Kingdom without God the Father. Jesus stated numerous times that everything the Father had was His, and everything He did as the Son of God was as a result of what the Father showed Him to do. *(John 5:19; 8:29; 16:15)*

5. The time has come and now is, where the Church will be full of sons and daughters who have been reconnected with the Father and are walking in their full Kingdom identity. *(Ephesians 5:27)*

6. We are taught to pray for Salvation and then to be filled with the Holy Spirit, but Jesus also said that He

would bring the Father back to live inside of us and make Their abode in us. *(John 14:23)*

7. We have assumed or most often been misinformed that everything in Salvation is ours by Grace, when actually it must be obtained by finishing our race. It is the race for sonship, or better defined as Transfiguration. *(Matthew 24:13; 1 John 3)*

8. The key to the children of Israel's heart posture was the same key that made mankind walk away from God the Father in the first place: Rebellion! The adversary, satan, tricked Adam and Eve by getting them to surrender their identity to him. He made them think that God was keeping something from them, and he offered them the same curse of rebellion that he himself had entered into as he separated himself from God the Father. *(Ezekiel 28; Isaiah 14)*

9. How will we know when we have passed the son test and that we have passed from being *qualified* to enter the race to be *verified* by Abba Father, Daddy God Himself? When you have been reconciled to the Father and He is in you and you are in Him. When the Father Himself shows up and confirms your sonship with signs and wonders following and you are doing what Jesus did and greater.

Prayer of Salvation

Heavenly Father, I come to You in the Name of Jesus. Your Word says, "Whosoever shall call on the name of the Lord shall be saved" *(Acts 2:21)*. I am calling on You, for I am a sinner. I have lived my life for myself only and no longer want to be separated from you. I repent and I decide from this day forward to turn from my ways. Jesus, I believe you died on the cross to save me. You did what I could not do for myself. I pray and ask Jesus to come into my heart and be Lord over my life.

I am now reborn! I am a Christian, a child of Almighty God! I am saved! You also said in Your Word, "If ye then being evil, know how to give good gifts unto your children: How much more shall your heavenly Father give the Holy Spirit to them that ask him?" *(Luke 11:13)*. I'm also asking You to fill me with the Holy Spirit. Holy Spirit rise within me as I praise God. I fully expect to speak with other tongues as You give me the utterance *(Acts 2:4)*. In Jesus Mighty Name. Amen.

Prayer of Sonship

Heavenly Father, I ask that you lead me by your Holy Spirit through revelation to enter into sonship. I pray not to live by grace alone but to move into the realm of faith. Help me to know you and your ways, that I may be in one mind and one accord with your spirit. I thank you for calling me to be your disciple and I pray to be among your chosen, the elect. I ask for revelation, understanding, insight, knowledge and wisdom that I may be transformed by the renewing of my mind. I pray for courage, boldness and a thirst for righteousness.

I yield to your chastening as I know your love for me will bring me to a place of perfection. I pray to walk in full alignment as a son to do those things that Jesus did and greater. I pray for the spirit of humility and a heart posture of knowing that I am nothing without you. Help me to position myself to receive my full inheritance and to fulfill the calling on my life. Release to me that which you have stored up for me, before the foundation of the world. Father, I want to be one with you and live the rest of my life and eternity as your son! In Jesus Name I pray. Amen.

Notes

_____

_____

_____

_____

_____

_____

_____

_____

_____

_____

_____

_____

_____

_____

_____

_____

_____

_____

_____

_____

Notes

_____

_____

_____

_____

_____

_____

_____

_____

_____

_____

_____

_____

_____

_____

_____

_____

_____

_____

_____

_____

_____

_____

Notes

_____

_____

_____

_____

_____

_____

_____

_____

_____

_____

_____

_____

_____

_____

_____

_____

_____

_____

_____

_____

_____

FATHERLESS

Closing Thoughts

There is nothing more beautiful than knowing that you have found what you have been searching for your entire life. Nothing could fill the void that was only destined for One to fill: the Father! Reconciling back to the Father was the moment that changed everything for me. All of the confusion, all of the pain, all of the longing had finally begun to be satisfied through each encounter with the Father. As He breathed on my hope again and the reason why I am alive, the world became much less frightening and a lot more exciting. He started to show me the possibilities that I didn't see before, how everything I had gone through began to look like a blessing and, most importantly, that I was no longer alone and an orphan but have been strategically set apart "for such a time as this" to glorify my Father. This is my purpose! In everything I do, my aim is that it may bring the most amount of glory back to the Father who never left me but was always by my side, excited for the abundant life that He predestined for me.

~*KM*

Now I understand that when you are a child of God, nothing is ever lost. Whatever is given to you is entrusted to you for a time, a reason and a season. God NEVER allows anything to be taken from you that He will not return to you multiplied with interest after you have successfully passed the test and endured the process *(Matthew 19:29; Job 42:12)*.

God our Father does everything excellently! While you are in the Valley of the Shadow of Death, sometimes it feels like you are not going to make it out. Some days you will feel like you are all alone and like nothing fits together or makes sense. This is where God the Father, God the Son and God the Holy Spirit show Themselves to you in a whole new way. This is where you realize that God is more than a church service, a song or an offering. This is where you realize that you are one of those who have been chosen to know God and be called His friend.

All of creation is groaning right now and waiting for the sons of God to be manifested and take their places upon the mountains of influence. We are those who seemed like we were in last place, forgotten and even forsaken by God. But we were not forgotten — we were hidden. We were separated and set apart for the Master's use. We are servants unto the world but set apart to be kings under the authority of the King of kings and Lord of lords.

Jesus is not only our Savior; He is our example. He is a seed that fell to the ground and was planted for me. He was planted so that I could be harvested. He was wounded so I could be healed. He was obedient to death so that I could live in His resurrection. Jesus is my hero! He is the greatest Superhero that ever existed on this planet.

Holy Spirit is my Comforter, Guide, Teacher, Personal Trainer and Best Friend, and I am 100-percent sure that I would not have endured everything that I have made it through without Him.

In this season of my life, I have come to discover that the missing link has always been the Father. Now being restored through salvation to Abba Father, Daddy God, I have been reacquainted with my Creator in whose image I was made. I now have my Kingdom ID card and realize that no matter what this world says, I was born and created for greatness.

I never really had a relationship with my earthly father because he was not around for more than a few days of my life. One day I realized that I had never lost or missed anything because my life was not like other people. I had actually been chosen to help heal those who were broken and in need of finding their purpose and destiny. Once I found the light of God's truth, no lie could ever hold me again. I realized that I had been chosen by God Himself to be His son. Chosen like Jesus to lay down my life and be a bridge for the lost to walk across. Chosen to shine bright as a light unto the world, so that every son could find his way back home and never need to be Fatherless.

~JCWIII

FATHERLESS

SOURCES

[1] Fathers.com/statistics-and-research

[2] U.S. Census Bureau. *Children's Living Arrangements and Characteristics*. Washington, DC, March 2011: Table C8.

[3] U.S. Department of Health & Human Services. National Center for Health Statistics. *Survey on Child Health*. Washington, DC, 1993.

[4] Hoffmann, John P. "The Community Context of Family Structure and Adolescent Drug Use." *Journal of Marriage and Family*, May 2002: 314-330.

[5] Hofferth, S.L. "Residential father family type and child well-being: investment versus selection." *Demography*, Feb. 2006: 53-77.

[6] Weitoft, Gunilla Ringbäck, Anders Hjern, Bengt Haglund, and Måns Rosén. "Mortality, severe morbidity, and injury in children living with single parents in Sweden: a population-based study." *The Lancet*, Jan. 25, 2003: 289-295.

[7] "rebellion." Google . 2019.

[8] "honor." Merriam-Webster.com. 2019.

[9] "courage." Merriam-Webster.com. 2019.

[10] "dunamis." Bible tools.org. 2019.

ABOUT THE AUTHORS

Kierra McKenzie

My name is Kierra McKenzie, and I was born and raised in Maryland. Family has always been a huge part of my life. I have been blessed to understand the life of being an only child of my mother and spending time on weekends with my six siblings from my father. I did not grow up with a hunger or curiosity for God, my early experience was going to my local catholic church every Sunday as a family tradition.

There was an experience in college where I sat in on a service at a Baptist church and during the alter call, I felt a pull to go to the altar but fought until the last minute. I immediately fell at the altar and began to weep uncontrollably. A lady stood praying for me, but I didn't hear anything that she said because I couldn't stop crying. Once I wiped my face, I got up and left. And that was that; I just went about my day. No one explained to me salvation, reading the Bible or even plugging into a church community. To me it was just another awesome experience, but I had absolutely no language for it.

After graduating college with a B.S. in psychology, I didn't know what direction I wanted to take my life into. I had been dancing since the age of three with different dance companies and apprenticeships, and that passion was stronger inside of me than my other passion to become a psychologist or counselor. So, I decided to move to L.A. to pursue my dream of becoming a dancer.

I began taking classes, performing in different dance

projects, commercials and acting gigs, while trying to survive as a server. I started going to a church — suddenly, I grew a hunger for more of God and started seeking out many questions like "Is God real?" and "What is my purpose?" I didn't even know that you could hear the voice of God! That's what intrigued me the most. Yes, I was one of those people that went to the alter at least 10 times just to be sure I was saved, until the Holy Spirit revealed to me that the encounter I had at the Baptist Church in college was my salvation. I began to serve in the church, became one of the lead ushers and joined their dance ministry.

Even though I had a great Father, I still grew up with attributes of an orphan spirit. God began dealing with the issues of my heart and childhood roots that I developed that needed to be broken down. I realized that it wasn't ok to want to be isolated or judge mental or selfish or self-centered. Without knowing it, I developed this survival mentality where I felt like I had to look out for myself and take care of "me" or who else will. Which caused me to live a life of self-preservation that was rooted in fear.

God reversed the enemy's plans for my soul and gave me hope and a future that I could never have dreamed of. God the Father was the answer to every void and misunderstanding in my heart. This journey isn't easy, but He predestined me with a plan of redemption that my cup may overflow and those who drink from it will receive the healing and medicine that I have qualified to become, through my testimony. I continue to walk the path that he has prepared for me and helping those he sends my way to realize that this life was never intended for you to do it alone but to walk with Him as a son or daughter and become one with the lover of your soul.

John C. Whitfield III

My name is John Whitfield, and I was born and raised in Washington, D.C. I served 11 years in the United States Army and another six years as a civilian contractor in Germany, Bosnia, Croatia, Kosovo, Macedonia, Korea, Afghanistan and Dubai. Using my gifts in media, music, audio/video production, content creation, instructional design and public speaking, I am taking the Gospel to Hollywood and to the entire world. My calling is to be a light unto the world.

I have a personal relationship with Jesus that I developed at an early age, getting saved at the age of seven and being baptized shortly after. I was filled with the most precious gift of the Holy Spirit at the age of 17, shortly after joining the U.S. military and arriving in Monterey, CA. I give total glory and honor to Christ, who causes His presence and anointing to invade everything that I say and do. "The Spirit of the Lord is upon me, because He has anointed me to preach the gospel to the poor; He has sent me to heal the brokenhearted, to proclaim liberty to the captives and recovery of sight to the blind, to set at liberty those who are oppressed; to proclaim the acceptable year of the Lord" (Luke 4:18-19).

I am currently working on my Doctorate in Apostolic Leadership and Applied Ministry. I speak in different locations when called upon, and I intentionally endeavor to "press toward the mark for the prize of the high calling of God in Christ Jesus" (Philippians 3:14)! I walk in all of the fivefold ministry gifts, highlighting whatever gift that God needs me to use at the time. I have a strong calling and passion to see God's sons realize their purpose, come into alignment with their destiny, and get equipped for the service of ushering in

God's Kingdom here on earth. I believe that the time is coming — and now is — when the last will be first and the first shall be last (Matthew 20:16). This is the season when the sons of God are manifested as we make our way back to God the Father and are restored.

Writing the book *Fatherless* with my dear and beloved Kierra McKenzie has been a love offering unto my Lord and Savior Jesus, and it is 100-percent divinely inspired by my very Best Friend, Holy Spirit. As you read this book, you will be set free, elevated and come into revelation after revelation of the Father's love.

Ministry Calling:

— Apostle, Prophet, Evangelist, Pastor and Teacher
— Entrepreneur, Instructional Designer, Content Creator and Audio/Video/TV/Radio Producer

Education:

— Associate of Science Degree in Recording Arts
— Bachelor of Science Degree in Entertainment Business
— Master of Science Degree in Instructional Design & Technology
— Master's in Apostolic Leadership and Applied Ministry
— Doctorate in Apostolic Leadership and Applied Ministry (2021)

Visit us at www.prolifickingdom.com for Courses, Webinars, Books, Coaching, Videos, Updates, and Prolific Content!

Made in the USA
Coppell, TX
25 March 2020